AUDREY COHEN COLLEGE
50664000110520
Rist, Georg, 1923-/Integrating vocationa
LB775 .S72 R48 C.1 STACKS 1979

D1686483

LB 775 S72 R48

Rist, Georg,
Integrating vocational and general education

DATE DUE

LB 775 S72 R48

Rist, Georg, 1923-
Integrating vocational and general education

| DATE | ISSUED TO |
|---|---|
| | FEB 2 4 1991 |
| | |
| | |

COLLEGE FOR HUMAN

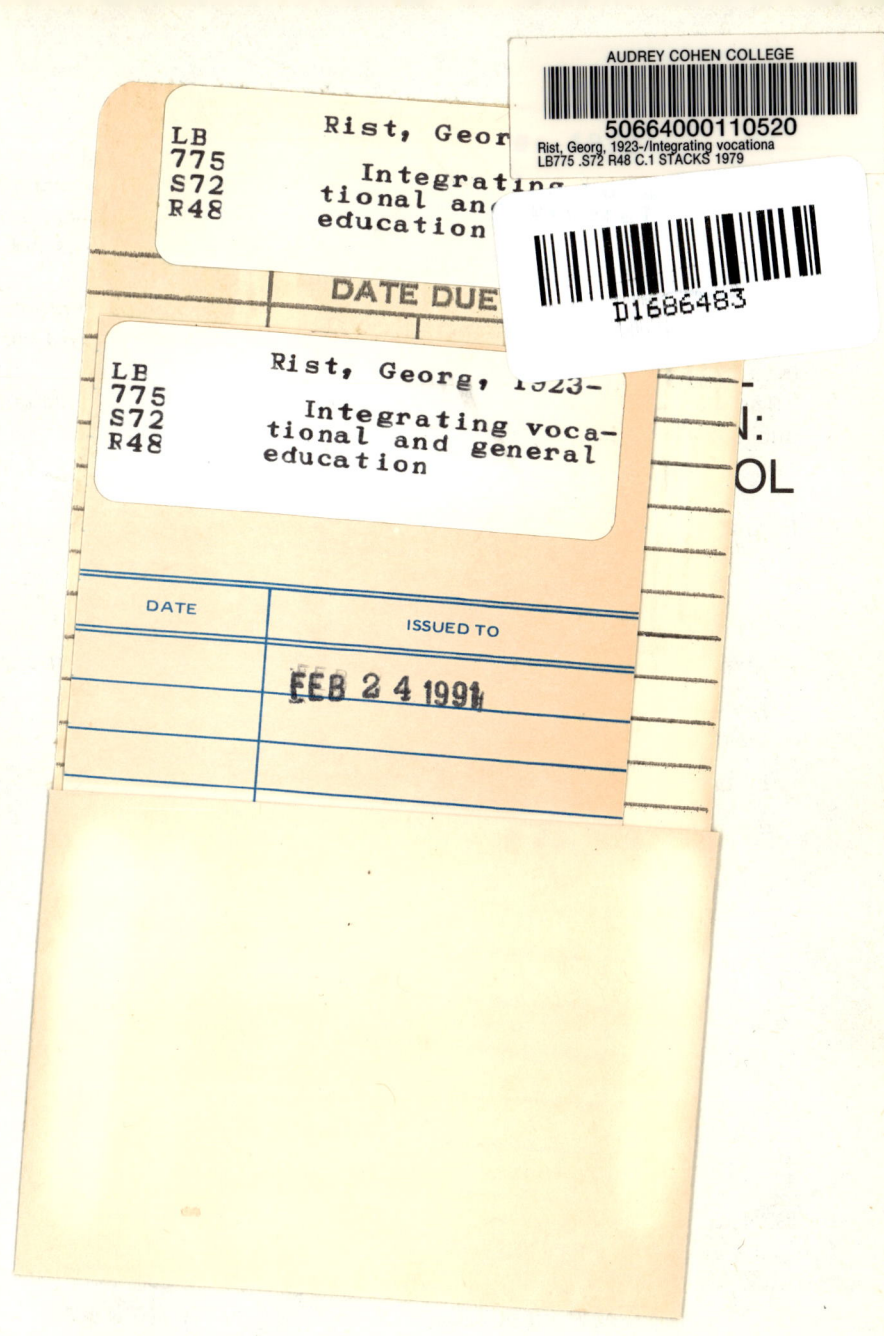

+LB775 .S72 R48

NEW YORK, N.Y. 10014

The Unesco Institute for Education, Hamburg, is a legally independent entity. While the programmes of the Institute are established along the lines laid down by the General Conference of Unesco, the publications of the Institute are issued under its sole responsibility; Unesco is not responsible for their contents.

The points of view, selection of facts, and opinions expressed are those of the authors and do not necessarily coincide with official positions of the Unesco Institute for Education, Hamburg.

The designations employed and the presentation of the material in this publication do not imply the expression of any opinion whatsoever on the part of the Unesco Secretariat concerning the legal status of any country or territory, or of its authorities, or concerning the delimitations of the frontiers of any country or territory.

An expanded version of this report is available in German under the title

**Die Hiberniaschule.** Von der Lehrwerkstatt zur Gesamtschule: eine Waldorfschule integriert berufliches und allgemeines Lernen.

by Georg Rist and Peter Schneider. Hamburg, Rowohlt, 1977.

ISBN: 92-820-1024-4

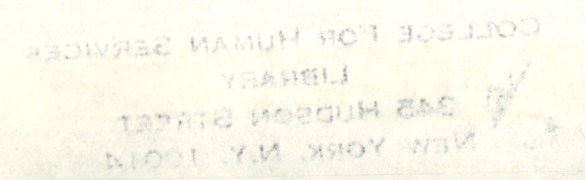

uie case studies 1

# INTEGRATING VOCATIONAL AND GENERAL EDUCATION: A RUDOLF STEINER SCHOOL

Case Study of the Hibernia School, Herne, Federal Republic of Germany

Georg Rist
Peter Schneider

1979

unesco institute for education
hamburg

uie monographs

1. **Lifelong Education and School Curriculum**
   by R. H. Dave
   (also available in French)

2. **Lifelong Education and the School**
   Abstracts and Bibliography
   (Bilingual — English and French)
   prepared by R. H. Dave and N. Stiemerling

3. **Reflections on Lifelong Education and the School**
   edited by R. H. Dave

4. **Lifelong Education,
   Schools and Curricula in Developing Countries**
   by H. W. R. Hawes
   (also available in French)

5. **Lifelong Education
   and the Preparation of Educational Personnel**
   by James Lynch
   (also available in French and Spanish)

6. **Basic Education in the Sahel Countries**
   by M. Botti, M. D. Carelli and M. Saliba
   (also available in French)

7. **Lifelong Education and Community Learning:
   Three Case Studies in India**
   by V. Patel and N. N. Shukla. W. van Vliet (ed.)

8. **Lifelong Education: A Stocktaking**
   edited by A. J. Cropley

9. **School Curriculum in the Context of Lifelong Learning**
   by U. Hameyer

CONTENTS

Foreword     xi

Preface     1

Chapter 1: THE EDUCATIONAL ORIGINS OF THE HIBERNIA SCHOOL     3
- 1.1   Sunday, 2 March 1975     3
- 1.2   The geographical and socio-economic environment of the School - an educational challenge     3
- 1.3   Orpheus and Eurydice: Opera as part of the curriculum     6
- 1.4   Development of the Hibernia School from factory training unit to an integrated comprehensive school with its own educational character     8
- 1.4.1   *Rudolf Steiner's approach to education. Historical background of the Hibernia School*     8
- 1.4.2   *From factory training unit to the Hibernia Education and Training Centre*     10
- 1.4.3   *Educational experiences in the Hibernia Education and Training Centre*     15
- 1.4.4   *From the Hibernia Education and Training Centre to the integrated comprehensive Hibernia School*     20
- Notes     24

Chapter 2: HIBERNIA SCHOOL EDUCATION IN PRACTICE     26
- 2.1   Remarks on the reports presented in this chapter     26
- 2.1.1   *The teacher's task*     27
- 2.1.2   *Educational conference work*     29
- 2.1.3   *Collegiate self-administration*     30
- 2.1.4   *Overall goals*     30

| | | |
|---|---|---|
| 2.1.5 | *Educational organization* | 30 |
| 2.1.6 | *The curriculum* | 31 |
| 2.2 | **The work of the class teacher in Grades 1-8** | 34 |
| 2.2.1 | *The main lessons* | 34 |
| 2.2.2 | *Fairy tales in Grade 1* | 38 |
| 2.2.3 | *The social aspect of a class community* | 40 |
| 2.2.4 | *Parents' involvement* | 43 |
| 2.3 | **The structure of practical education in Grades 1-8 or 9** | 46 |
| 2.3.1 | *Principal issues in practical education* | 46 |
| 2.3.2 | *Knitting lessons in Grade 1* | 47 |
| 2.3.3 | *Needlework in the early grades* | 49 |
| 2.3.4 | *Baking bread in Grade 3* | 49 |
| 2.3.5 | *False romanticism in education?* | 50 |
| 2.3.6 | *Knitting a pair of socks in Grade 5 needlework lessons* | 51 |
| 2.3.7 | *Clay modelling and wood carving in Grade 5* | 52 |
| 2.3.8 | *Dolls and soft toy animals in Grade 6 needlework lessons* | 53 |
| 2.3.9 | *Gardening instruction in Grades 5-9* | 54 |
| 2.3.10 | *Forestry work in Grade 7* | 58 |
| 2.3.11 | *The development phase of 13 and 14 year olds* | 59 |
| 2.3.12 | *Woodwork in Grades 7 and 8* | 61 |
| 2.3.13 | *Basket-weaving in Grade 8* | 63 |
| 2.3.14 | *Copperwork in Grades 8 and 9* | 64 |
| 2.3.15 | *On handicraft work in Grades 7 and 8* | 66 |
| 2.3.16 | *Healthy movement education in gymnastics* | 66 |
| 2.3.17 | *Eurhythmy lessons at Hibernia School* | 68 |
| 2.4 | **Grades 9-10** | 70 |
| 2.4.1 | *Psychological development in the adolescent phase* | 70 |

| | | |
|---|---|---|
| 2.4.2 | *Articulation and diversification of the curriculum* | 71 |
| 2.4.3 | *Class community and change of direction* | 72 |
| 2.4.4 | *Psychological development through practical activity* | 72 |
| 2.4.5 | *Character training through work with iron, copper and wood* | 73 |
| 2.4.6 | *Curricular goals of the practical activities* | 74 |
| 2.4.7 | *Blacksmith's work* | 75 |
| 2.4.8 | *Locksmith's work in Grade 9* | 79 |
| 2.4.9 | *Grade 9 make wooden boxes* | 80 |
| 2.4.10 | *Electrical work in Grade 9* | 81 |
| 2.4.11 | *Chemistry block period in Grade 9* | 82 |
| 2.4.12 | *Drawing and painting lessons in Grades 9 and 10* | 83 |
| 2.4.13 | *Locksmith's work in Grade 10* | 85 |
| 2.4.14 | *Machine operation in Grades 9 and 10* | 87 |
| 2.4.15 | *Vocational studies in Grade 10. Industrial processes* | 88 |
| 2.4.16 | *Mathematics and surveying in Grade 10* | 89 |
| 2.4.17 | *Toy making in Grade 10. Dolls* | 92 |
| 2.4.18 | *Poetry block period in Grade 10* | 93 |
| 2.4.19 | *Dramatics in Grade 10* | 95 |
| 2.5 | **Grade 11** | 100 |
| 2.5.1 | *Learning in the social domain* | 100 |
| 2.5.2 | *Practical period in the kindergarten as part of social development* | 106 |
| 2.5.3 | *Work in a hospital* | 108 |
| 2.5.4 | *Practical experience in a large-scale chemical plant* | 111 |
| 2.5.5 | *Study of Parzival in Grade 11* | 112 |
| 2.6 | **Grade 12** | 115 |
| 2.6.1 | *Preparation for maturity* | 115 |

| | | |
|---|---|---|
| 2.6.2 | *The training of pre-school teachers* | 116 |
| 2.6.3 | *Electrical installation* | 118 |
| 2.6.4 | *Economic studies* | 119 |
| 2.6.5 | *Art lessons. Modelling a human head in clay* | 123 |
| 2.6.6 | *Joint appreciation of work done in art lessons* | 125 |
| 2.6.7 | *Producing a piece of work for the certificate of apprenticeship* | 127 |
| 2.7 | Parents cooperation in an independent school | 129 |
| 2.8 | Financing, legal status and organization of the Hibernia School. Collegiate management and self-administration | 133 |
| 2.8.1 | *Financial position* | 133 |
| 2.8.2 | *Legal status of the Hibernia School as an independent school* | 135 |
| 2.8.3 | *Internal organization* | 136 |
| Notes | | 142 |
| Chapter 3: | EDUCATIONAL ASPECTS OF RUDOLF STEINER'S "STUDY OF MAN" AND THEIR APPLICATION IN THE HIBERNIA SCHOOL | 144 |
| 3.1 | Development phases and the changing nature of learning | 144 |
| 3.2 | Differentiation in the process of becoming a complete human being, need for comprehensiveness and specificity of learning provision | 146 |
| 3.2.1 | *The interrelationship of theory and practice and the pedagogical significance of art* | 146 |
| 3.2.2 | *Differentiation in individual and social learning* | 148 |
| 3.2.3 | *Memory, imagination and creativity* | 149 |
| 3.3 | Growth to full humanity as self-realization | 150 |
| 3.3.1 | *The cultural development of humanity and the role of learning* | 150 |
| 3.3.2 | *Necessity of development-specific learning provision. The issue of age-relatedness* | 151 |

| | | |
|---|---|---|
| 3.3.3 | *Education for freedom. From guided to self-directed learning* | 151 |
| 3.4 | Principles deriving from the special approach of the Hibernia School | 153 |
| 3.4.1 | *Art and craft work as preliminary stages of a technical education* | 153 |
| 3.4.2 | *Practical skill, usefulness and necessity are basic elements of technical education* | 154 |
| 3.4.3 | *Age-relatedness in the practical components of education* | 157 |
| 3.4.4 | *Possibilities of integrating theoretical and practical learning* | 163 |
| 3.4.5 | *The principle of ability promotion and its effect on achievement* | 167 |
| 3.5 | Outcomes of training in learning competence. Curricula vitae of ex-pupils | 172 |
| 3.6 | Applicability of the Hibernia School concept to the national school system | 181 |
| 3.6.1 | *Staff, parents, financing* | 181 |
| 3.6.2 | *Preconditions for adopting the Hibernia School concept* | 182 |
| 3.6.3 | *Reconsideration of the role of the state* | 183 |
| 3.7 | Prospects. Lifelong learning and the reform of society | 184 |
| Notes | | 186 |
| Appendix: SCHOOL REPORT | | 187 |
| Bibliography | | 191 |

# FOREWORD

Of the many educational principles which together constitute the concept of Lifelong Education, <u>articulation</u> is the one most frequently mentioned. The term articulation is used, for example, to refer to coordination between different agencies involved in education, to integration between the successive phases and objectives of the education process, and to links between the several subsystems, services and institutions which are components of the overall education system.

In the context of the school, curriculum articulation refers to the relationship of learning objectives, content, methods and materials within a particular grade, to the organisation of parallel grades or streams, and to the degree of continuity between grades, between educational levels, and between the school curriculum and educational influences outside. The recent publication of the Unesco Institute for Education, <u>School Curriculum in the Context of Lifelong Learning</u> by Uwe Hameyer, surveys the literature on articulation of the school curriculum, reviewing the theory and practice which supports and clarifies the principles of Lifelong Education. The present study complements this by describing and analysing a school where the aim of curriculum articulation in its essential vertical and horizontal dimensions has been successfully converted into actual practice.

The Hibernia School attracted the attention of the Institute by the exemplary way in which three major components of the curriculum, i.e. artistic, practical and academic education, are articulated. From the very first grade up to grade 13 these three major areas are given almost equal emphasis, with the result that, at the end of their time at school, every pupil is potentially qualified to enter either university or skilled technical employment.

The Hibernia School curriculum is heavily influenced by the educational philosophy and practical pedagogy developed by Rudolf Steiner. It is open to speculation whether the form of curriculum articulation exemplified here could be implemented independently of Steiner's theory. The study illustrates a specific aspect of curriculum articulation, thereby contributing to the clarification of the concept in general and providing practical hints of how the articulation may be achieved. Such an example may also be of use to schools not sharing the philosophy of the Steiner Schools.

The preparation of this report has been a joint venture in many respects. I would like to express my particular appreciation to the two authors, who despite their heavy teaching commitments have been able to conduct this study so successfully. They themselves would like to be considered as the representatives of the staff of the Hibernia School on whose joint contributions the whole study is based. Originally published in German for an audience familiar with and sympathetic towards Rudolf Steiner Schools, the report had to be translated, abridged and adapted to suit the international audience to which the publications of the Unesco Institute for Education are addressed. It was the skill of the translator-editor, Mrs J Kesavan, as well as the cooperation of the two authors which produced the present text. The Unesco Institute for Education is pleased to include the Hibernia School in its series of educational case studies as a complement to the several theoretical studies and literature surveys conducted on the topic of lifelong education.

M. D. Carelli
Director

PREFACE

The Hibernia School was not designed on a drawing board nor planned "from above". Rather it has developed, step by step, in the course of 25 years of activity (1). This development from a factory training unit to a comprehensive school has been oriented throughout by continuous and direct communication with the societal and social environment. The school conception of education is reflected in a curriculum in which practical, artistic and academic learning are equally represented and integrated. In the course of a "stimulating correspondence" between the authorities and the Hibernia School, the concepts of "work study" (2) and "basic vocational school" have crystallized and have been adopted by the national education system of the Federal Republic of Germany. These developments are described in Chapter 1.

When in the early 1970s UNESCO turned its attention to the problem of how lifelong learning could be established, it looked for institutions and concepts in the various national education systems that could serve as examples. The Hibernia School seemed to offer a suitable model which had the special advantage of a good many years of experience. Hence the Unesco Institute for Education, Hamburg, requested the Hibernia School to describe its educational activities as well as the pedagogical theory underlying these methods. The teachers' reports presented in Chapter 2 are, therefore, of a "workshop" nature. They attempt to give the reader as direct as possible an insight into the many educational "workshops" held in the school. These reports follow the method practised in Waldorf education of describing factual situations, characterizing them and keeping them flexible rather than limiting them through definition. For reasons of space it has been found necessary to concentrate on the course in practical education.

Our warmest thanks go to all the colleagues who contributed these reports.

Chapter 3 is devoted to the methodological and conceptual premises and rationales of the Hibernia School. An attempt has been made to show that the anthropological foundations of Rudolf Steiner's educational theory, on which its pedagogical concepts are based, are highly relevant to the problems dominating current discussion on educational policy. It is hoped that this exposition will contribute to an understanding whereby the Hibernia School will be included among the models to be considered in devising a reformed education system, as an example of a concept that, on the one hand, enables every pupil to expand all the facets of his physiological and psychological potential in accordance with his individuality, and on the other hand, that refrains from selection by social or ability criteria.

This book could not have been written without the sympathetic support offered by colleagues, collaborators and friends of the Hibernia School. The Rex Roth Foundation for Work Research of the Association of German Industry Foundations has provided essential financial support. Dr. Klaus Fintelmann, Arbeitsstelle für Bildungsforschung, Bochum, Mr. Hartmut Zeither, Max-Planck-Institut für Bildungsforschung, Berlin, and Mr. Werner A. Moser, Basle, have assisted us in many details. In particular, Dr. Fintelmann, founder and for many years head of the Hibernia School, has been able to answer many questions concerning the school's history and conception of education. Dr. Ruth Moering has helped to prepare the manuscript and has improved it through constructive criticism. We are deeply indebted to them all.

Georg Rist
Peter Schneider

NOTES

(1) As explained in Chapter 1 of this book, existing Waldorf school concepts offered no model for the special concerns of the Hibernia School. It had to evolve its own answers to the new educational challenges. Thus it has realized many of the principles Rudolf Steiner had demanded as early as 1919, but which had not yet been put into practice in the Waldorf schools.
(2) "Arbeitslehre" defined by the German National Education Committee as "practical activities accompanied by interpretation and reflection", providing "education for participation in the modern working world".

CHAPTER 1

THE EDUCATIONAL ORIGINS OF THE HIBERNIA SCHOOL

1.1   Sunday, 2 March 1975

   As usual, clouds of smog billowing from the cooling-towers of the power-station pollute the air. From a nearby chemical factory streaks of rust-coloured nitrose fumes drift across the school site, even on this late Sunday afternoon. But next to the deserted nineteenth century distillery and the large house tottering from subsidence in the mines below, the packed car park suggests that something special is happening. So do the crowds of people in their Sunday best who are pouring into the wide, funnel-shaped forecourt of the Hibernia School. They make for the entrance hall, whose big windows open onto the greenery of the large inner courtyard. The Hibernia School is throbbing with first-night fever. In a few minutes the Gluck opera *Orpheus and Eurydice* is going to be performed, set to the school's own choreography, which is based on eurhythmy (1) and gives the chorus a dramatic role, with music by the school orchestra. The auditorium goes quiet. The curtain rises, the orchestra, at floor level in front of the stage, strikes up the overture. Pools of blue and green light appear, gradually intensifying. Then the chorus enters. While some kneel down along both sides of the proscenium in the shape of a shell, others surround Orpheus as he laments the disappearance of his Eurydice.


1.2   The geographical and socio-economic environment of the School - an educational challenge

   A large part of this first-night audience, pupils, parents and guests, live in this area between chemical factories, mines, the power station and the school in the most densely populated region in Europe. The adults who work in shifts in these industries, including night shifts, feel the contrast between the noise, the harshly rationalised nature of their everyday jobs and the colours, harmonious sounds and movements of the performance which the pupils are staging.

Roughly one thousand children attend the School. The youngest go to the kindergarten, the oldest will, after 14 years of schooling, acquire a genuine dual qualification, a certificate of apprenticeship, for instance in machine fitting or carpentry, and the secondary school leaving certificate. This integration of academic, artistic and technical education on the basis of Rudolf Steiner's education theory is what gives the Hibernia School its special character. It is an integrated comprehensive school of its own kind, in which the principle of equal opportunity is made a reality through an all-embracing and versatile system of promoting talent.

The school is embedded in an industrial civilization typical of the Ruhr area. Some two thirds of a mile to the northeast are the acid towers of a nitrogen works, less than half a mile away the cooling towers of the Shamrock mine. This non-privileged geographical location is reflected in the socio-economic data provided by parents and pupils. A preliminary survey in February 1976 of the 700 homes represented in the school showed the following levels of occupation:

- 27%  workers such as miners, fitters, welders, skilled chemical workers, railwaymen, electricians;
- 43%  middle-level civil servants and employees such as master craftsmen and foremen in the mining and construction industries, inspectors, engineers, technicians;
- 18.5% self-employed such as commercial agents, craftsmen, shop-keepers;
- 9%   professional occupations, such as doctors, lawyers, architects, teachers;
- 2.5% others (orphans, students) (2)

and the following levels of education:

- 50%  approx. had left school after the basic statutory period;
- 38%  approx. had completed intermediate secondary education (general secondary school, technical school or college of technology);

12%     approx. had completed academic secondary
        education and gone on to university.

These figures reflect the social objective of the School, namely to be a *community school* for children from *all social strata in its catchment area.*

Admission of pupils is therefore guided by the principle that the composition of each class should roughly correspond to the social structure of the surrounding industrial area. The parents' economic situation plays no part in the admission or non-admission of a pupil. The School sees it as one of its tasks also to enrol children from difficult social backgrounds. But one precondition must be met: parents registering their children must explicitly declare their readiness to cooperate with the School.

The pedagogy and the organizational structure of the School are determined by what is necessary for a child's development in an industrial conurbation. The parents who live here, their socio-economic circumstances, and the teachers in the highly specific position of a school that started as a factory training unit form the framework in which the School finds its identity.

In the same way that the surrounding architecture is determined by the technical demands of production, the architecture of the School is likewise based on the children's needs. To quote Klaus V. Fintelmann who was closely involved in drawing up the plans:

> "The buildings are so arranged that the tensions and the organizational pattern inherent in the educational structure become visible and can be experienced. For instance, as you go in, the classrooms for academic lessons are opposite the workshops; the older pupils' recreation area is partly enclosed, encouraging the pupils to stroll more contemplatively, while the younger children's play-ground, although connected to the other area by the Hall, is more open and suited to games. The Hall, where the entire School comes together as a community every day for lunch and at special functions, is at the centre of the whole compound. These basic themes are reinforced by the architectural design of other parts of the building,

as well as by selected works of art. They are
continued in the shape and colour schemes of the
classrooms, corridors and workshops. A school
building conceived in this way enables the pupils
to become really aware of each other, to meet;
it becomes a true living-space for the children."
(3)

A glance at the overall structure of the School leaves the
impression of a compact stance towards the exterior, thus creating a sheltered educational space within. Its location and
design symbolize, on the one hand, its coherence with the surrounding industrial civilization, and on the other the intention
not to let these outside influences penetrate uncontrolled into
the educational sanctuary of the School.

This principle was also a motive for the School's *move
from the Hibernia Mining Company's nitrogen factory to new
premises in December, 1963*. It puts a few hundred yards distance between the pupils and the unremitting harshness of a
big industrial concern, to which they had until then been
directly exposed. Situated outside the factory, though still
right within the industrial area, the School became a more
effective place of shelter. The Hibernia School had transferred
part of the technical working world it had just left into its
*own workshops*. But contact with that world was never interrupted. On the day following the move, pupils went back to the
factory for the session of industrial work which is part of
their curriculum, but now they were coming from, and returning
to, the shelter of the School. It was now not only a spiritual
and temporal refuge - efforts had been made to build that up
even within the factory - but also a physical one.

1.3   Orpheus and Eurydice:  Opera as part of the curriculum

Weeks before the first-night the Hall was turned into an
improvised theatre. Amid a jumble of upturned tables, folding
chairs and music stands, some 50 musicians practised and tuned
their instruments. On the two wide staircases leading to the
stage roughly 120 pupils from Grades 8-12 in colourful batik
robes chattered and milled around. On the proscenium, 10 figures
in blue overalls hammered and soldered away, while up above you
could see legs apparently swinging in space as their owners
installed the new lighting system. In between all this the
eurhythmy group tried to get some of its sequences right.

Then, at a given signal, all was quiet. The "workmen" stopped, those wearing costumes knelt down to form a dancing group, the musicians played the slow introduction, and the 120-strong chorus intoned the lament. The orchestra, the chorus, the eurhythmy group, the lighting operators, all would have to react so promptly and naturally that the happenings on the stage would come alive to the audience. Again and again the scene was rehearsed until each participant would feel that the individual efforts of 200 people were merging into a whole.

The chorus was used as a dramatic person - not merely a singing background but an active participant, accompanying the action with rhythmic and expressive gestures. It required a high degree of discipline, empathy and sense of form for each individual to act dynamically within a group, to fulfil himself only as a group member.

The costumes for the chorus were designed, cut out and sewn by the pupils themselves in their needlework lessons. Plain cotton cloth donated by parents was tie-dyed in red, violet and blue - an inexpensive solution which made a splendid and expressive tableau.

The stage sets were based on designs which the pupils had studied in their drawing and history of art lessons. The sets were made in the school workshops, and many hours were spent assembling them on the stage. The entirely new type of lighting system, thought out by the handicraft teachers together with the 11th grade pupils, was installed by the pupils themselves. They worked on their own, using their own initiative, and themselves traced and corrected faults. The result was a lighting system producing subtle blends and shades of colour. The continuous play of varieties of colour on the upper, lower and side ramps of the stage, while the centre and front were flooded in white and two shades of green, produced a spiritually expressive effect, turning the dramatic and musical performance into a struggle between the realms of light and darkness.

Opera in school is a means of harnessing artistic and manual work to achieve an educational end: the development of the pupils' creativity and willpower in their entirety in the serene, spiritual and expressive medium of music.

A project of this kind highlights some central objectives of the Hibernia School:

- Educationally justifiable targets of achievement are to be chosen by the pupils themselves and reached by their own efforts. The satisfaction of seeing a successful outcome to their intensive and persevering efforts leads to the setting of new standards.

- The cross-fertilization of several areas of the curriculum - in this case choreographic notions acquired in music and art lessons in combination with the technical skills learnt in the school workshops - and their integration into a total education which will foster each pupil's talents and abilities in a manner suited to his age.

- The integration of a learning process which is comprehensive, polyvalent and above all close-to-life. It should take place in various settings (workshop, stage, eurhythmy-room), comprise various types of content (planning and installation of a stage lighting system, Greek mythology in German lessons, significance and effects of colours in painting lessons), and create varied social learning situations. Inspired by the example of the older pupils, the younger ones can set themselves new aims.

These are the principles which lead the Hibernia School to assigning equal importance in its curriculum to academic, technical and vocational elements, so that when pupils leave school they are able to lead a life of independence and self-responsibility. School experiences are designed to be a help towards lifelong learning.

1.4 <u>Development of the Hibernia School from factory training unit to an integrated comprehensive school with its own educational character</u>

1.4.1 *Rudolf Steiner's approach to education. Historical background of the Hibernia School*

The Hibernia School originated from Rudolf Steiner's attempts to put his social ideas into practice in the years after the first World War. He considered the following questions important for the national educational system:

- How must both individual schools and the entire education system be organized and how must they operate to avoid creating social divisions?
- How can the school initiate a lifelong learning process in such a manner that the future adult will be able to comprehend new problems, solve them independently and thus live as a lifelong learner?
- What must be the teacher's social commitment, and in what kind of free educational situation must he work, so as to be an example of lifelong learning to his pupils? Steiner maintained that teachers can communicate only what they themselves practice.

In this sense the economic, legal and cultural structures of the social order at that time were to be transformed on the basis of the notion of liberated man. The result was to be a differentiated structure with relatively autonomous cultural, economic and legal sectors. The school as a part of the cultural sector was to be freed from economic dependence and legal restrictions; its methods and curricula were to be developed solely on the basis of the pupils' needs. Steiner's aim was the all-embracing promotion of every individual's development, up to the age of 18, irrespective of his social status. Consequently the school was designed as a comprehensive school, i.e. for all children, with no selection mechanisms such as differentiation by ability, repetition of classes, or marking systems. In talking of *all* children Steiner particularly had in mind the 80% who were working-class children and who, at that ime, left school at 14 years of age. The first Waldorf School, founded in 1919, was primarily intended for children of workers at the Waldorf-Astoria cigarette factory in Stuttgart. These working-class children lived in an action-oriented environment, including their own home, in which practical abilities were valued more highly than was the case in the verbally-oriented culture of the middle class.

According to Steiner's basic concept practical activity ranked on a par with academic learning. He regarded practical work as being of very great educational value. But in the first Waldorf School in Stuttgart he could only partially implement these principles. Although a comprehensive artistic and practical education for every child was initiated in the pre-school classes, existing political conditions and legislative barriers made it impossible to achieve the integration of vocational-technical training and general education he had aimed for. Shortly before his death in March 1925 he said that the Waldorf School must change course. He was no longer able to explain what exactly he meant by that, but it seems certain that he was referring to a reorientation of the School towards greater emphasis on artistic and practical education.

Eight years later, in 1933, the National Socialists stopped the expansion of the ten Waldorf schools then existing in Germany by imposing a ban on enrolment of further pupils. Later they closed the schools one by one.

When in 1945 the Rudolf Steiner school movement was able to start up again, new schools - far exceeding in number the old ones that had been closed - were established within a few years in many parts of the Federal Republic of Germany. Due to this rapid expansion, the original Stuttgart school was used as a model for the new ones. In addition to the school movement, educational work based on the same pedagogical goals was started for adolescents who had already begun their working life as apprentices. An industrialist closely connected with the Waldorf School movement introduced general education into the training programme for apprentices in his furniture factory. Other industrial firms followed his example. One of these was the Hibernia Mining Company's nitrogen factory.

1.4.2 *From factory training unit to the Hibernia Education and Training Centre*

At that time 70 apprentices in the nitrogen factory were being trained as fitters, mechanics, lathe operators, or electricians. K.J. Fintelmann, the initiator of the new scheme, started teaching them academic and artistic subjects within the training period. But it soon became clear that the intention to develop the pupils' critical judgment and creative behaviour conflicted with the conventional industrial training where the apprentices were expected to work immediately according to given measurements and norms, with the objective of attaining technical perfection. They only learnt to carry out what others had already laid down in technical drawings, and they were given no chance of developing their own imagination and initiative.

Another obstacle was the virtual absence of any previous

practical education of these adolescents. Our contemporary civilisation offers very little if any opportunity of learning through the medium of practical work, such as wood-chopping, digging, hoeing, barrowpushing, coal-shovelling, fire-making, laundering, keeping small animals, or agriculture. The young people began their apprenticeship as "technical illiterates". Was it right to confront them immediately, unschooled as they were in motor or craft skills, with the highly specialized techniques of manual work and the rationality of norm-oriented production?

When these two shortcomings had been recognized, doubts also began to grow about the value of existing vocational-technical training, and the question arose how such training could be designed so as to foster the all-round development of human capacities and abilities. This implied a change in the original aim. What was required was not a further extension to but a qualitative transformation of the existing on-the-job training of apprentices. Three aspects of this question were investigated:

- Are there preliminary stages for learning technical behaviour, in other words, a form of practical education that would lead from children's play to technically prescribed work?

- Is there an educational link between the development of certain human qualities (practical qualities such as perseverance, reliability, spontaneity) and training in occupational activities?

- How should the methods and didactics of a curriculum of technical education be designed to correspond to this educational, non-vocational aspect?

For vocational training this meant devising a basic training course founded on an artistic approach and aiming to engender a wide range of practical abilities before concentrating on the skills required for a specific occupation. The vocational aspect would gain from the development of general abilities such as dexterity, versatility, accuracy, reliability, perseverance, etc.

The following basic crafts were chosen:

- woodwork (from carving artistic forms to accurate joinery)
- copper beating
- smithing.

This selection (4) was made because:
- these crafts lend themselves to a balanced, differentiated, all-round practical education enabling the pupils to continue learning all the time in the practical and vocational domains;
- they involve varied, intensive physical activity and call for full but differentiated use of physical strength;
- they train adolescents in versatile manual skills as well as in character traits such as accuracy, perseverence, spontaneity, etc.

This transformation of a practical training course into education through practical work had repercussions on the general and vocational, academic and artistic lessons: "general education", originally intended to be merely an "extra", and vocational education now permeated each other and merged into one.

As a result of the educational insights gained in the course of this process, the following changes were introduced:
- It was possible to postpone the choice of an occupation until the end of the first year of training (9th year of schooling), subsequently even until the middle of the 2nd training (10th school) year. This postponement helped the pupils enormously in making a really suitable choice; one might even say that it was impossible for them to do so any earlier. In this period of 1 or 1 1/2 years the teachers got to know the adolescents well in their day-to-day work. They became familiar with the problems involved in choosing an occupation, they acquired an appropriate basis for evaluation and could then really advise the pupils. The adolescents, for their part, had an opportunity to try themselves out, also in other technical courses that have not yet been mentioned; they

were older now and could develop preferences on the basis of their own experience.

- As the three areas of education (practical, artistic, academic) carried and supported each other, *a more economic pattern of educational activity* was achieved. In their artistic and craft work the pupils could orient, activate and concretize their thinking by the objective logic of technique and craftsmanship. On the other hand, their theoretical education helped them to understand work-processes and techniques and increased their learning abilities in the practical field.

- The efficiency of this mutual support and stimulation from the three educational areas was raised even further by the introduction of a timetable on the pattern shown in Figure 6 (see p.60). After 2-3 hours of theoretical lessons - including vocational studies given by the workshop teachers, which were thus fully integrated into the system - the apprentices had 1-2 hours of art lessons followed, after school lunch, by 3 hours of practical work.

In this manner the apprentices were first required to exercise and school their *thinking ability*. Next their *artistic sensitivity and expression* was stimulated, and finally they had to engage in intensive *physical activity*. It was found that this daily rhythm increased their desire to learn, and that the daily craft work trained their continuity and perseverance. Thus the foundation had been laid for the rhythmic alternation between mental and manual-physical activities in the Hibernia School timetable.

The temporal as well as didactic interaction of the various areas of the curriculum resulted in an entirely new and more economic pattern of educational activity. The adolescents were offered a far more comprehensive education than they could obtain over the same period of time via a conventional training programme. Eventually it was even possible to reduce the number of hours required per day and to introduce holiday periods in excess of the legal requirement. A crucial reason for this was that in each of the three areas the lessons covered only the time span in which adolescents are able to

concentrate fully.  Ineffective learning periods caused by
strain on one faculty or by working too long on one single skill
or subject had been cut out.  This arrangement provided a transition, adapted to the development of the adolescent, to the 8-hour working day of the adult with which the 14 to 15 year old
school leaver had until then been abruptly confronted.

    An appropriate *educational organization* was developed.
It profited from the existence of relevant patterns in Waldorf
School education, in particular its *block period principle*.
This was applied to the technical and artistic subjects in
their new context.  Block period means that a certain subject
is taught, or an artistic or craft activity engaged in, at the
same time every day (e.g. 7.45 to 9.25 a.m.) for a certain
period (3-4 weeks), at the end of which it is discontinued for
several weeks and then resumed, again in the form of block
period lessons.  Thus a period of very intensive concentration
on a subject is followed by a period of "forgetting", in the
sense of a fertile creative break during which this controlled
forgetting has a beneficial effect on the learning process.
New aspects, new insights, grow "by themselves" - for the new
block period.  However, such a block period must have an internal shape, for example a beginning, a peak and an end.  For
academic lessons this implies that within the period the pupils
must get to know a specific, structured and rounded field of
knowledge.  For technical and artistic education it means that
an object or work of art must be completed and a certain technique be learnt in that period.

    The development from merely adding academic and artistic
education to the practical training in the workshop, to a new
artistic instruction found its definitive expression in an independent educational organization.  In view of the effect
these three curriculum areas had on the adolescents by reason
of their integration, a virtually equal number of hours was
allotted to each of them.

    This new conception of education was worked out in the
years 1953-1956, and the training unit was given the name of
Hibernia Education and Training Centre.

### 1.4.3 *Educational experiences in the Hibernia Education and Training Centre*

Vocational training seen as *Menschenbildung* (education of human beings) emerged ever more clearly as the basic idea underlying the whole conception of the Hibernia Education and Training Centre. Education of human beings was understood to mean the generation of *lifelong learning processes* - at that time especially in the vocational field - rather than a cumulative addition of pre-determined knowledge and skills. Thus the fundamental conception of Waldorf education, "How can the school transmit skills and knowledge in a manner which will bring about an all-round education of human beings", was also applied to craft, technical and vocational learning.

As even the Rudolf Steiner school movement offered virtually no model for this concept, it was necessary to construct adequate answers for this new educational situation out of the basic elements of Steiner's educational theory. A decisive factor in this endeavour was a willingness to learn from the Centre's own educational approach. Experiences were evaluated, their implications for further development were clarified, and in this way little by little new, significant insights were won.

The application of the didactic principle of block periods may serve as an example. The question arose whether block periods have significance also for practical instruction. But how many hours per day should be set aside for it, how many weeks should a block period last, how long should be the interval between periods? Is there any significance in what other subjects are studied in the intervals, whether other objects are worked on, other techniques practised? All this was tried out, evaluated and modified.

The assumption that the block period principle is also valid for practical learning was confirmed by a surprising *increase in learning intensity*. This results not only from the stimulation of having many new starts and from the pleasure given by new objects produced within a relatively short time, but primarily from the "fruitfulness of a break". During the time a newly learnt discipline is not practised but is allowed to "rest", the skills acquired in it grow, becoming freer, more independent and innovative. At the beginning of a new block period the pupils always possessed greater ability in a particular discipline than they had had at the end of the previous period.

This development took place under the very critical eyes of the factory workers, the works council, the management and the parents. All of them, though open to new ideas and methods, wanted to see realistic and demonstrable results. These were achieved in considerable number and provided an impetus for making even more far-reaching changes. In weekly meetings the ongoing experiments and intended changes were discussed, analyzed and developed. Through this common work the instructors, the teachers of academic subjects and the art teachers of this training unit grew together into a unified teaching body.

The first one-week educational seminar was held at Easter 1957. It deepened the shared educational insights and worked out new sets of problems to be investigated. At the same time artistic exercises (painting, drawing, clay modelling) were included - an element that had already played a major role in the education of the apprentices themselves. This stimulation of a common awareness proved so fruitful that an educational seminar has been held at Easter every year since. An *intensive learning process* thus came into being which covered both the task of educating apprentices and the new form of co-operative work which it implied.

The new educational insights which were gradually acquired and put into operation had a decisive influence on the conception of the Hibernia School as an integrated comprehensive school. They are therefore summarized in the following sections.

a) General practical education

In trying to design a practical fundamental education which would not only equip the pupils with the abilities required for a specific future occupation, but would also prepare them for learning it, the question arose: Which future activities can be built on those learnt earlier? It was found that versatile practical and manual skill, combined with agile thinking, can considerably reduce the period of specific training. Although in the final school pattern approx. 70% of instruction time was devoted to "general learning" and only 30% to specific vocational education, the results of Chamber of Commerce and Industry examinations in vocational knowledge and skills were not inferior to those previously attained. On the contrary, they were slightly better - an unexpected outcome (5). Practical education was organized *in two stages*:
1) *general practical education,* justified by the resulting increase in learning ability in the practical as well as in the academic domain.

The first stage may be subdivided as follows:
- *play* combined with movement training;
- *doing something practical* (needlework, gardening);
- specialized *handicraft* work;
- *practical* vocation-oriented work and production.

2) *Learning of specific vocational knowledge and skills.* This is now done with the aid of the learning ability previously engendered. Learning such knowledge and skills shows the adolescent how he or she can gradually master the requirements for a specific occupation - a process that can be repeated many times in their future lives. In keeping with changing industrial developments, the decision on what occupation to choose loses some of its importance: it becomes a preliminary decision about a *first job* instead of being a final decision for an entire lifetime. (6)

Thus a course of practical education was developed, in which the stages follow in as consistent a sequence as do, for instance, the learning goals in the taxonomy of a cognitive curriculum.

b) Didactic coordination of the learning settings (classroom, workshop, factory floor)

The expansion of vocational training into a general practical education made it possible for theory and practice to be closely interrelated and for the learning content to be reallocated to the various learning settings and teaching personnel. In vocational learning, for instance, a differentiation was made between skill-related knowledge, mediated by the workshop teacher in the workshop, and general insights, which are better worked out in the classroom. Calculation of volumes, weights, percentages, prices, divisions, cutting speeds, etc. were assigned to the workshop, the place where the adolescents are confronted with these matters in their concrete working situations. Practice in such *situation-related thinking* is of special importance for future reality-oriented theoretical work and reformist activities. It builds a foundation for *creative thinking*. Theoretical vocational instruction given in the classroom by the workshop teacher after the practical work forms a link between practical and academic education.

If the company workshop was to be used as a learning location, it was necessary first to interest members of the company's work force in these educational tasks and to secure their cooperation. These contacts between training workshop and school, and between company and workplace, also provided many constructive suggestions and grounds for mutual understanding. They prevented the innovative development of workshop and school from going its own way and becoming divorced from reality.

c) The societal aspect of vocational learning

To accustom the adolescents to concrete, real-life work, the objects they were asked to make were invariably things for actual use, never conventional "practice" pieces. *Usability* became the paramount criterion. The pupils were trained to correct any mistake they had made in such a manner that the object concerned could still be used. Furthermore, what they produced had not only to be *usable*, it had to serve a need, its production had to be *necessary*. The adolescents had to experience the fact that in the contemporary production process with its division of labour nobody makes a product by or for himself; he always works in cooperation with others and for others. It was found not only possible but indispensable for educational reasons to give adolescents only concrete, real-life tasks, even when their vocational learning took place in special educational settings, and training for a specific occupation was the main objective. This principle was later taken over by the Hibernia School.

d) Age-related learning objectives and methods

Relating learning objectives and methods to age is of paramount importance in Rudolf Steiner's educational theory and developmental psychology. Hence a major concern in the conception of a practical education scheme was the age to which the various practical and vocational activities should be related. An attempt was made to find out whether certain *forms of activity* correspond to the adolescent phase in human development, what significance attaches to the *materials* used, etc. The outcomes of these efforts have already been referred to in the description of the concept of a practical general education and its stages.

Many insights could only be gained as a result of experimentation. The question of which was the right moment for adolescents to begin working in a commercial concern as part of their further training may serve as an example. Initially, they started in the second training year (10th year of school). But it soon became obvious that the 16 year olds could not bring sufficiently realistic critical judgement to bear on the social situations arising in the factory. Though they possessed a certain self-assurance regarding the work as such, they were unable to cope with the social ritual at the factory, with its jokes and deliberate embarassment, its authority structures and hidden hierarchies. They took at face value a lot of provocation that was merely intended to bring a person out or to establish contact. As a result of experiences of this kind, factory work was deferred for one year to the third year of training, now the 11th school year. By that time the 17 year old apprentices were capable of assimilating their experiences because their critical judgement was more mature and they were relatively more independent in their work. They were helped by the fact that in the meanwhile the School had learnt to prepare them not only for their work, but also for the social relations they would have to face in a factory.

The experiences acquired in the process of integrating practical-vocational, artistic and theoretical education may be summarized as follows:

1) It was found that the *adaptation of learning objectives, their didactics and methods, to the needs of the young according to their anthropological and psychological development*, in other words the *age-relatedness* of all learning, including vocational training, led to increased *learning motivation*.

2) The *didactic coordination* of the learning setting, i.e. factory work place, school workshop and classroom, made it possible to make all learning processes *lifelike*, directly related to reality. The areas of experience involved demand self-responsibility in the young people and relate their learning to *life in society*, which is necessary at that age.

3) Seeing and checking the products of their practical work exercised the adolescents' power of evaluation, and so schooled them in *realistic thinking and judgement*.

4) A new *teaching hygiene* was developed. Alternating types of work, changing foci in lessons, and block periods resulted in a new *timetable rhythm*.

5) The most important outcome of an all-round and age-related learning concept was that the adolescent acquired both *learning ability* and *learning optimism* as a basis for *lifelong learning*.

### 1.4.4 *From the Hibernia Education and Training Centre to the integrated comprehensive Hibernia School*

#### a) The new self-concept

The original intention of providing apprentices, not only with vocational training, but also with academic and artistic instruction adapted to their phase of development, had led to a new conception of vocational training as a whole, in which the non-vocational areas necessary for overall development were fully integrated. It was no longer a matter of improving the existing form of vocational training but of replacing it by a concept appropriate to the requirements of our times. The working world of an industrial society is constantly changing, demanding of the worker the ability to continue learning throughout his life. The primary task of contemporary vocational training is, therefore, to develop such *educability*. This goal was at the core of the learning concept of the Hibernia Education and Training Centre.

*Three consequences of this re-orientation.* The most important developments resulting from the re-definition of vocational education were *government recognition of the Education and Training Centre as an experimental school*, the *separation* of the new institution from an industrial company, and a *rounding off of its educational concept*.

In 1957/58 the Hibernia Education and Training Centre was recognized as an experimental school by the Ministry of Culture of North-Rhine-Westphalia. It was approved - in anticipation of future developments - as an *integrated* "Berufsfach-" and "Berufsaufbauschule" (7), that is, as an institution combining in one educational system an education which could until then be obtained only by attendance at two (or many more) separate establishments.

The new school was called *Hibernia Basic Vocational School*. This name was chosen to indicate the *new concept*, namely to replace training for a specific occupation by fundamental *education for lifelong educational learning*.

Recognition as an experimental school had far-reaching effects. For instance, the school was authorized to hold its own *school leaving examinations*. This enabled it to follow its educational principles to their logical conclusion.

One of the basic ideas in the new examination concept was to give every pupil the opportunity of showing that he *could do something*. The *examination*, the preparation, execution and evaluation of which extended over several weeks, was in itself a *learning process*; self-evaluation and courageous self-presentation had to be practised and perfected.

The work to be done for the examination varies in volume and degree of difficulty according to the individual's learning achievements. He himself makes the preparations for this task, carries it out and then *orally* presents and justifies both the object he has made and his procedure. This evidence of competence in his discipline is central to the entire examination procedure, with proof of other qualifications grouped around it.

This new examination concept solved an increasingly important problem that had arisen with the conventional examinations held by the Chamber of Commerce and Industry. At Hibernia the adolescents had been taught to pay attention to the social nature of their work; they had always produced objects that were needed. But in the Chamber of Commerce and Industry examinations they were required to make mere practice pieces, with no other function than to demonstrate their skill. The new examination concept in which each candidate chooses his own task encourages him to believe that everybody can make something that is usable and necessary in the life of his society.

b) <u>Independent sponsorship and management</u>

On becoming an independent school in 1959/60, the Hibernia School had to free itself from dependence on an industrial company. The principle of self-responsibility and participation demanded that the School be run by those immediately involved. Accordingly, a *School Association* was founded by parents, teachers and others ready to cooperate. Individuals and groups willing to support the educational concept of the Hibernia

School formed a *League of Friends of the Hibernia School*. Finally, a *Hibernia School Foundation* was established to ensure that the accruing funds would be used for the School's own purposes.

The step to financial and legal independence presented a great economic challenge. Workers who had previously received public assistance for the education of their children were now asked to make financial contributions towards a new school building. And this at a time when an adequate number of apprenticeships, entailing financial assistance for parents, were still available elsewhere. However, as a result of the educational work already done, the demand for places at the Hibernia School did not decrease; on the contrary, it increased considerably.

c) Expansion into a comprehensive school

The legal and economic autonomy which the school now enjoyed, permitted a further extension of its educational structure. This was done in two stages:

1) Expansion of the "basic vocational school" into an establishment for vocational education in line with contemporary conditions. This was accomplished in 1961 by the inclusion of social and educational occupations and, consequently, by the admission of girls. The schooling period was extended to 4 years.

2) Expansion into a comprehensive school encompassing the learning processes of childhood and adolescence as a whole. This concept stemmed from two convictions:

    - that many of the practical courses ought to start much earlier, some of them even at nursery school;

    - that an all-round education interrelating theory and practice is necessary for every young person, also - even particularly - for those who want later to study for a profession.

This expansion had three implications:

- Construction of a school building (1962/64)

which would itself serve as a learning aid supporting the new concept. This could be achieved only through considerable involvement of parents, pupils and teachers and through the understanding of the general public.

- Organisation of a collegiate management and self-administration as is implicit in the basic notion of an independent school. In the Hibernia School this collegiate management deals with all the tasks facing an independent school, from the day-to-day administration to management of its overall finances, from appointing personnel to developing new educational concepts. Guided by the principle of initiative and rotation of all tasks and functions, the management style of the School is inseparably bound up with lifelong education (see 2.8.3).

- Although the Hibernia School had been to all intents and purposes a fully integrated comprehensive school since 1964, legally it was a mere bundle of separate decisions by the authorities. In 1971 it was finally recognized as a comprehensive school of its own kind.

It is now an integrated comprehensive school providing pre-school, first level primary, and "Hauptschule" (8) education, technical/social and general upper secondary sections; its leaving certificates entitle the holders to enter a skilled occupation, a technical school, a College of Technology or Social Studies, and a university or university-level institution.

The following is a summary of the historical development of the Hibernia School:

1952-56 Establishment of the required learning settings and situations in the training workshop and factory organisation. Development and tryout of the overall concept of the Hibernia Education and Training Centre.

1957-58 The Ministry of Culture recognizes the institution under the name of *Basic Vocational School Hibernia* as an integrated full-time vocational school and vocational extension school.

1959-60 Detachment of the school from the Hibernia-Chemie company and foundation of an *Independent School*.

1961 Extension of the *Basic Vocational School* through addition of social studies and admission of girls.

1962-64 Erection of own school building.

1964 Extension by addition of grades 1-8 and a kindergarten. State approval as a first-level primary school and "Hauptschule".

1966 Further extension by addition of a "Studienkolleg" (general secondary education leading to university entrance).

1968 Upon request of the *Association of Parents of Thalidomide Children* and of the local authorities, establishment of a special education course for 26 such children.

1969 Introduction of collegiate management and self-administration.

1971 Official recognition as a *Comprehensive School of its Own Kind* combining first level primary school, Hauptschule, full-time vocational school, vocational extension school, advanced technical school, pre-school teacher training centre and institute of further education leading to higher education.


NOTES

(1) Rudolf Steiner's art of movement, not to be confused with eurhythmics (see 2.3.17).

(2) A comparison with a survey made in August 1968 reveals the following changes: the proportion of workers had fallen from 37.9% to 27%, that of self-employed had risen from 11.8% to 18.5%, while that of middle-level employees and professionals had hardly changed. This development corresponds to shifts in the population structure of the town of Wanne-Eickel (now Herne 2), characterised by a sharp decline in the proportion of industrial workers.

(3) Fintelmann, K.J.: "Entstehung und Aufbau der Hibernia Schule". In *Pädagogik heute*. (1.2.1969). Special issue.

(4) Because of external constraints it was not possible to include building and agricultural work.

(5) See Lübbers, K.H.: *Die Berufsausbildung im Rahmen der traditionellen betrieblichen Ausbildung eines Großbetriebes und im System der Hiberniaschule*. Düsseldorf: 1972. This investigation shows that on average Hibernia pupils achieve better results in the certificate of apprenticeship examination ("Gesellenprüfung") than do those trained in the training workshops of large concerns. It should also be mentioned that 50% to 65% of Hibernia pupils leaving after 12 or 14 years' schooling obtain the qualification for university or technical university entrance. Most of them have, in addition, acquired the qualification for entering a skilled occupation. The parents of roughly half these pupils have themselves had basic compulsory schooling only. This new pattern of education clearly promotes equality of opportunity.

(6) See p. 172 Curricula vitae of ex-pupils.

(7) A "Berufsfachschule" is a full-time vocational school on completion of which an examination for the certificate of apprenticeship or for qualification as a skilled worker may be taken. - The "Berufsaufbauschule" (vocational extension school) has by now been largely replaced by the "Fachoberschule" (advanced technical school or advanced school for social work). This leads to acquisition of the qualification for entry into a College of Technology.

(8) A "Hauptschule" covers the second period (5 years) of compulsory education following the first level primary school (4 years). It has no entrance examination and is the school type attended by the majority of German children, especially those not aiming at a semi-professional or professional career. On completion of the "Hauptschule", however, transition to institutions of advanced learning is possible after passing the relevant examination.

CHAPTER 2

HIBERNIA SCHOOL EDUCATION IN PRACTICE

2.1   <u>Remarks on the reports presented in this chapter</u>

The reports and examples of lessons included in this chapter have been written by experienced Hibernia School teachers. In this description of the School's teaching practice the emphasis is on areas in which the articulation of general academic, artistic, practical and vocational learning provision can be most clearly seen. Such comprehensive articulation is one of the cornerstones of the Hibernia School's concept of education. It is a preparation for lifelong learning.

The first step in the School's development from a factory training unit to the Hibernia School was the introduction of educational activities most unusual in a training programme for future fitters, lathe operators, electricians and chemical workers. They were taught watercolour painting; they rehearsed a play on an improvised stage; they talked about the structure of the earth in geology lessons; they studied skeletons in biology lessons to discover the difference between human and animal limb formations, especially the differences in the construction of instruments for gripping and walking, and the resulting differing potentialities of man and animal.

The present practice is an extension of this method. A 16-year-old future doctor, lawyer, teacher or educator stands at a work-bench filing a joint for the hydraulic power-drive of a dredger; future mechanics carefully paint layer upon layer of thin watercolour to produce glowing pictures. What is the purpose of this combination of theoretical, artistic and practical education?

Such variety of learning stimuli promotes an all-round expansion and individual development of the pupils in their thinking, feeling and will; it leads to human maturity. It also results in clear successes in examinations, but it would be a grave misunderstanding to assume that this is the actual aim.

These educational insights derive from Rudolf Steiner's understanding of the development of children and adolescents as worked out in his "Study of Man", on which the collective research done by the Hibernia School teaching staff is based. They see themselves as a group of teachers endeavouring to find answers to contemporary educational problems through practical application of Steiner's findings and methodological suggestions. Starting out from day-to-day practical experiences, their continuous joint study leads to an ever more differentiated knowledge of the development of the young, and this shared knowledge guides their educational activities. This close relationship between research and verification of the results in daily praxis characterizes Hibernia School education.

Teaching thus becomes a continuous learning process for the teacher as well as for the pupils. The teacher constantly learns from the lessons for the lessons. Such open-minded, flexible work oriented by the given situation is an essential feature of Rudolf Steiner's "art of education". The pupils, who see the teacher always adjusting his teaching to their needs, always learning, acquire an ability for lifelong learning - first, at the stage when they learn by imitation, by following the teacher's example, later by reflecting upon this practice, analyzing it and giving it a theoretical foundation so that it becomes an instrument they will be able to handle as adults, each in his own way.

A goal as comprehensive as this cannot be reached merely by providing lessons. It requires a school organisation entirely directed towards this end. This organisation can best be described by considering its various components.

### 2.1.1 *The teacher's task*

The interrelationship of the tasks shown in Figure 1 may best be illustrated by a particular case. At an educational conference, the subject of discussion was Grade 11, in which the pupils must decide on the subject area in which they want to specialize at school in preparation for their future occupation. It was agreed that several weeks of practical training in relevant institutions, such as kindergarten, industrial

## Interconnection of Teacher's Activities

Teacher's Tasks:
- (1) Educational Conference work
- (2) Curriculum
- (3) Further Development of Educational Organization
- (4) Collegiate Self-Administration
- (5) Talks with Parents
- (6) Work on Global Goals
- (7) Study of Non-School Problems

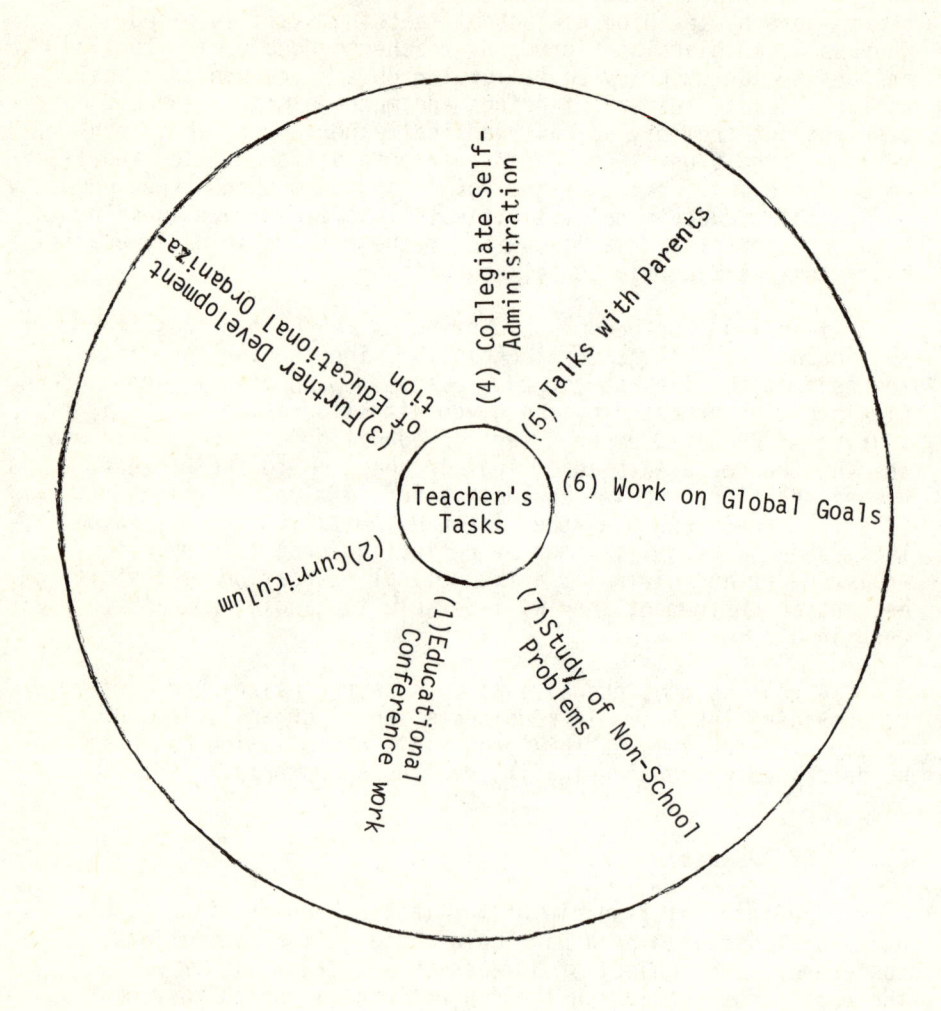

FIGURE 1

plant, hospital, etc. were necessary, and that those immediately concerned should take the decisions regarding the educational programme (1), its objectives within (2) and insertion into (3) the curriculum, and the assignment of its practical implementation to individual teachers (4). At a preparatory meeting the parents agreed to the plan and declared their readiness to cooperate (5). In the general conference discussion on the overall aims of the project (6) emphasis was laid on bringing the pupils into contact with the contemporary situation regarding employment and social conditions. This signifies a further step beyond the self-concept of the Waldorf School towards an institution created and constantly developing in answer to contemporary problems (7).

In the educational conferences the teaching staff have constantly to re-think the curriculum and the organisation of Waldorf education in the perspective of its global goals. Collegiate administration and cooperation with the parents' committees also affect everyday school practice. The teachers' relations with parents from widely differing social backgrounds already eliminate any risk of isolation of the School from the outside world. In addition, the School deliberately increases contacts with its social environment by means of various special events and festivals.

It has, regrettably, not yet been possible for the Hibernia School to put into effect Rudolf Steiner's suggestion that class teachers, after leading a class for eight years, should have a year's leave to engage in non-school activities, in order to participate actively in social development and changes in entirely different fields. They must, therefore, keep up by their own efforts their interest in what happens in public life, their interest in the world outside, which is one of the preconditions of fruitful teaching.

2.1.2 *Educational conference work*

A continual exchange of experience takes place at the weekly Educational Conferences attended by the entire staff, and at meetings of a number of groups entrusted with special tasks. Criteria suggested in the "Study of Man" serve as starting points for observation of individual pupils and classes. Listening to the judgement of others, each teacher expands and corrects his own, and joint processes of critical reflection and depersonalized consideration are engendered. These may crystallize into resolutions and decisions which, going beyond any particular problem under review, are always concerned with the School as a whole. This joint work of all teachers creates a fertile soil for the further development of curricula adapted to changes in the society or in official educational policy.

### 2.1.3 *Collegiate self-administration*

The particular responsibility structure of the Hibernia School (as of all Waldorf schools) is built on the conviction that all teaching activities are of equal value. It would be a direct contradiction of this principle if a hierarchical structure and bureaucratic rules were imposed from outside. How a school should be organized and administered is best decided by those who have to implement the decisions in the day-by-day school activities. Only they are in a position to validate or revise them in accordance with practical experience.

### 2.1.4 *Overall goals*

"Human dignity is inviolable" (Basic Law of the Federal Republic of Germany; Article 1, paragraph 1), and "every individual has the right to free development of his personality" (ibid.; Article 2, Paragraph 1). This interpretation of man fully applies to the child from his earliest age and determines the goals of Waldorf education. Educational and psychological procedures centre around the child or adolescent as a human being in his own right. They aim to provide him with a free area in which he can experience his individual and social gifts and the development of his corresponding abilities. In his thought, feeling and will his ego-disposition should grow into an ego-identity through the processes of individualization and socialization. Attention to body-mind interaction, and careful adaptation of learning contents and methods to his age, will help him to develop healthily and, when adult, to have forces at his disposal which will enable him to engage in a socially effective lifelong learning process.

### 2.1.5 *Educational organization*

The principal factor determining the organization of educational provision is not the learning content but the method of education. There is a fundamental difference between the so-called block period lessons, in which one subject or area is focussed on for several weeks and then left to rest for some time, and the continuity of regular lessons. To give an example: in gardening instruction in Grades 5 and 6 it is considered specially important for the pupils to experience the annual cycle. Instruction is therefore given in regular lessons. From Grade 7, when the pupils are able to do more intensive and differentiated practical work, they have block period lessons in which complete selected tasks are carried out.

Continuous practice is necessary for learning foreign languages. They are, therefore, taught in regular lessons, whereas subjects such as history, geography, and chemistry are taught in block periods. In German and mathematics new themes are dealt with in block periods and practised in regular lessons. The rationale and practice of block periods have been described in detail in Chapter 1 (pp. 14 and 15).

Great importance is attached to the right sequencing of theoretical, artistic and practical lessons in the course of the day. The central didactic principle is to give all lessons an artistic design by emphasizing the How rather than the What. Vivid, situation-related communication with the pupils takes precedence over achievement-related learning goals. The varied gifts of all pupils can thus be utilized for the benefit of the whole class. This presupposes classes with a heterogeneous achievement level. There is no repetition of grades; the pupils remain together as a unit throughout their school life.

This organization of education has been worked out, and is kept flexible, by the teachers' conferences and collegiate self-administration. Even the architectural design described in Chapter 1 was developed by the architect in constant close cooperation with the teachers.

2.1.6 *The curriculum*

The curriculum is oriented by the development and abilities of the child at every age. This is exemplified by Figure 2 (Distribution of Practical Activities over the School Years). As an example of the vertical articulation of teaching subject and method, the sequencing of woodwork instruction is shown in Figure 3.

## Distribution of Practical Activities over the School Years

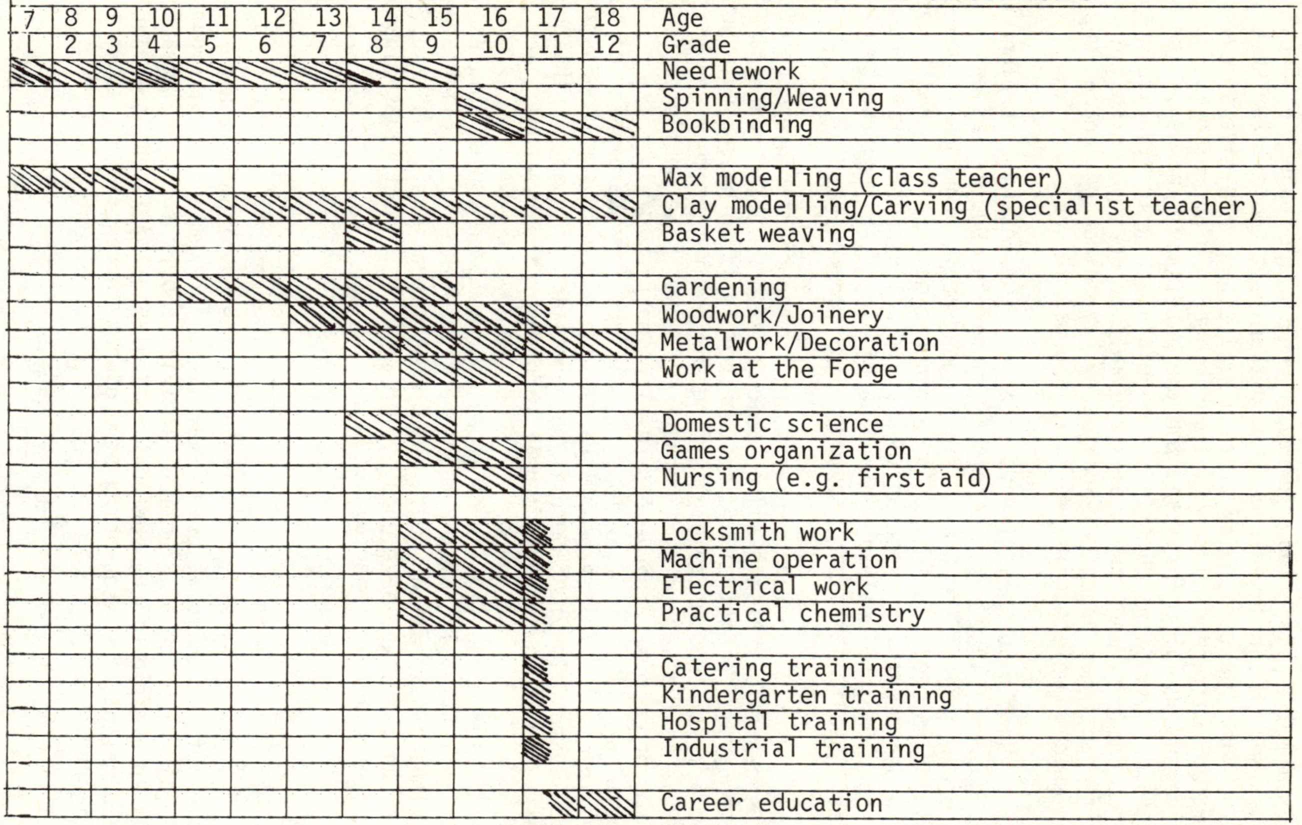

| Age | 7 | 8 | 9 | 10 | 11 | 12 | 13 | 14 | 15 | 16 | 17 | 18 |
|---|---|---|---|---|---|---|---|---|---|---|---|---|
| Grade | 1 | 2 | 3 | 4 | 5 | 6 | 7 | 8 | 9 | 10 | 11 | 12 |

- Needlework
- Spinning/Weaving
- Bookbinding
- Wax modelling (class teacher)
- Clay modelling/Carving (specialist teacher)
- Basket weaving
- Gardening
- Woodwork/Joinery
- Metalwork/Decoration
- Work at the Forge
- Domestic science
- Games organization
- Nursing (e.g. first aid)
- Locksmith work
- Machine operation
- Electrical work
- Practical chemistry
- Catering training
- Kindergarten training
- Hospital training
- Industrial training
- Career education

FIGURE 2

Vertical Articulation of Woodwork Instruction with Psycho-Physical Development

| Age | Development Stage | Activities Corresponding to Students' Development Stage | Examples of Pieces of Work |
|---|---|---|---|
| 18 — 17 — | Awakening need for social responsibility (combination of social with personal aspects) | Independent work based on understanding of the whole field of woodwork<br><br>Work in a social context; teamwork | Desk as apprenticeship examination piece (p.128).<br>Pieces of furniture made to order |
| 16 — | Desire for specialized criteria | Work requiring specialized competence and knowledge. Exact joinery | Dovetailed medicine chest |
| 15 — 14 — | Ability to form own judgement oriented by factual and material aspects, and desire for detachment to find own identity | Work in which the objectivity of matter as indicator of specialized competence and accuracy can be experienced. Opportunities for self-correction through independent checking and measuring of own work. Planing, sawing | Box with insets (p.80) e.g., tool or shoe polish box, flower stand, mechanical wooden toy, simple garden stool |
| 13 — | Awakening ability for abstraction. Ability for and artistic activity to specialized more differentiated understanding of purpose-sawing, wood splitting, chopping. The relatedness of an object is clamped into the vice. and of first specialized Rasping, sanding working techniques. More detachment from environment | Work facilitating transition from play and artistic activity to specialized activity: cutting with scraper, exact sawing, wood splitting, chopping. The object is clamped into the vice. Rasping, sanding | Bird-table. simple toys. Firewood, practical forestry exercise (p.53, 58).<br>Darning egg, cooking spoon, planting sticks, carving of simple animal figures |
| 12 — 11 — | Developing physical and manual skills calling for handling of new materials such as wood | Whittling of pieces of wood held in the hand | Carving curves to produce simple animal shapes, such as hedgehogs, elephants, rabbits (p.52) |

Curriculum (Wood)

FIGURE 3

Figure 4 shows the horizontal structuring of the curriculum for Grades 1-6. As will be seen, intellectual demands are always combined with handwork and physical (movement) education. The first two hours of the day are occupied by the so-called main lesson, a special kind of block period lesson given by the class teacher. In these main lessons the subject of the period is taught within a rhythmically arranged pattern of speech, music and, particularly in the lower grades, movement practice. Then follow the regular lessons held at the same times every week. Right from the first grade these include foreign languages (English and Russian). In Grades 1 and 2 all children learn to play the recorder, in the third and fourth grades a stringed instrument such as the violin. Rhythmic changes involving all the pupils' faculties in turn prevent strain through one-sided demands on body or mind. They stimulate the child's diverse energies enabling him to express himself creatively in many domains. But the stimulus never comes to the individual in isolation; fruitful development can occur only in his relationship with the social group, the class community.

In the following pages, working reports by Hibernia School teachers are presented as examples of the School's educational practice. The selection is based on pupils' ages and on insights gained from developmental psychology (vertical articulation), with emphasis on examples where the way of combining handicraft-occupational, academic and artistic education is most typical of the Hibernia School (horizontal differentiation). In their style and formulation of concepts the reports also illustrate how the personality of the teacher determines the manner in which he translates the ideas of Waldorf education into practice.

2.2  The work of the class teacher in Grades 1-8

A class teacher remains in charge of his class from Grade 1 to Grade 8 inclusive, giving the majority of lessons himself.

2.2.1 *The main lessons*

Like all other block period lessons in the Hibernia School, the main lessons consist of 3-4 week periods - longer in the first three grades - in which the same curricular subject (German, mathematics, history, geography, nature study) is taught every day. Their distinguishing feature, already outlined in paragraph 2.1.6, is that they form a composite unit.

Example of Curriculum from Grades 1-6

| | Monday | Tuesday | Wednesday | Thursday | Friday | Saturday | Time |
|---|---|---|---|---|---|---|---|
| Block Periods | English | Russian | Main Lessons | | | Painting | 7.45 |
| | | | English | Russian | English | Russian | 9.40 |
| | Wax or Clay Modelling | Music (Instrumental) | Needlework | Music (Singing) | German or Maths (class teacher) | Gardening | 10.35 |
| Regular (Practice) Lessons | Carving | Religion | Needlework | Religion | Music (Instrumental) | Gardening | 11.30 |
| | Music (Singing) | Eurhythmy | Gymnastics | Eurhythmy | Gymnastics | | 12.10 -13.05 |

FIGURE 4

The rhythmic flux this design creates is comparable to the process of breathing in and breathing out. Though the time span devoted to the components of this process changes with the children's age, the fundamental pattern remains constant. All main lessons start with musical exercises on simple instruments. such as the recorder, lyre, chimes, and with singing and recitation. In Grade 1, beat and rhythm are emphasized by clapping, stamping, knocking, while in the fourth grade the alliteration of the *Edda*, to give an example, imposes its own forceful rhythm. An eighth year class is already capable of reciting Goethe prose texts in the pupils' own vocal style.

These exercises, which challenge the will and stimulate feeling, are followed by the subject lesson of the block period, leading to observation and reflection. It first takes up the theme that had been communicated the day before in the form of a picture or story, that is as an experience. What the children remember is now put together, ordered and channelled into a kind of appreciation, according to the age of the class. Next a new theme is communicated as an experience. For instance, if in a fourth grade animal study lesson the cow was the subject one day, this theme is recapitulated and raised to the level of reflection the next day - occasionally also for several days running - and then a very different animal is introduced, for example a lion whose powerful running and leaping capacities call for a dramatic description. His body, living habits, environment, his position in the animal world make a colourful picture which the children enlarge from their own imagination in the subsequent conversation until the teacher gives it a new direction. Now that the children have been appealed to in their whole being, they are quite eager to get out their exercise books and convert the thrill into activity. They paint or draw the lion or write something about him. The atmosphere in the classroom becomes relaxed. Advice is sought from neighbours, crayons are exchanged. This practice activity is used as a basis for homework, usually optional in the lower grades. Later, when the pupils have become used to performing regular duties, it should be accepted by all.

Then follows a different (learning) area: the daily story (see 2.2.2).

This pattern may be considered typical of many other rhythmic processes in Grades 1-8. In the early grades more time is devoted to musical-rhythmic exercises. Later, in recitation, the content receives more emphasis, and the selected items increasingly contain an element that stimulates thought and contemplation. In the subsequent regular lessons also the main stress is on pictorial or descriptive communication appealing to the will and to feeling, with just a modicum of detached contemplation. For up to the age of 8 or 9 the child experiences the world essentially as a whole of which he himself is a part. He wants to grasp it, so to speak, with hands and feet, with his entire body. Writing, for example, is learnt by first pronouncing the letters, running them as shapes, forming them with arms and hands, before they are developed from pictures into alphabetic characters - like hieroglyphics. Similarly, multiplication tables are "incorporated" by means of running, hopping or clapping.

Towards the end of the third school year the pupils expect a different teaching language, one that is stronger and more sober, yet at the same time more emotionally differentiated. At that age they feel confronted with the world, and they want to know exactly what it is like. In general knowledge lessons they now learn something about the basic forms of housebuilding and agriculture, in animal and nature study they learn about living habits and natural growth. But their feelings must still be strongly engaged; they must still "experience" before they can comprehend. They need to "grasp" in the literal sense of the word.

At around twelve years of age children begin to feel the need for recognizing causal connections. The harmony of their bodily movements is now disturbed by faster bone growth and, as a result, a heavier body. Outward roughness and the oversensitivity of their awakening individual emotional life signal the approach of puberty.

At this stage of growing awareness of their own body mechanisms they can also begin to understand the laws of nature in physics and chemistry, geology and astronomy. These disciplines speak an objective language in which the pupils can exercise their awakening critical judgment. From merely drawing geometrical forms they now advance to geometry proper. Abstraction in mathematics and understanding of grammatical relationships are practised. In history, geography and literature, too, processes and inter-connections are studied. Reading of German texts leads to an elementary study of literary style.

The eight years spent together end with a theatrical performance. Plays by Shakespeare or Schiller, Hebbel, Raimund,

Lope de Vega and others, adapted for school performance, are suitable for the purpose. Sometimes a teacher dramatizes an appropriate prose text especially suited for the particular character of his class. Everybody's skills and experiences are needed for the rehearsals, costume making and building of stage sets, and each pupil studying and rehearsing a role is involved in his whole being. The abilities thus called forth constitute a genuine development of the personality far exceeding any that can be achieved by accumulation of knowledge. They place powers of will, feeling and thought at the disposal of each pupil, irrespective of his gifts, that will benefit him in his future life. This is the educational purpose of dramatic performances by the class.

Rosemarie Bütow

## 2.2.2 *Fairy tales in Grade 1*

Story-telling occupies an important place in the Waldorf School curriculum. It is articulated with the main lessons and other block period lessons. Up to Grade 8 it accompanies the children throughout the year like the theme of a piece of music from which all its variations flow. It leads from fairy tales in Grade 1 via fables, legends, biblical stories, mythology and the sagas of the Germanic Peoples, the Greeks and the Romans, to ethnological stories and thence to a description of the races and peoples of the world in Grade 8. In Grade 5, it links up with the first history lessons. In Grade 4, animal study connects up with the animal fables told in Grade 2. Thus story telling lays a pictorial basis for all subjects. This method is justified by the fundamental educational insight that everything a human being is to conceive clearly at any stage of life must first have been experienced by the child. Such experience is provided by stories which impress pictures on the child's imagination, pictures that continue to inspire him, that he can continue to enlarge. From Grades 4-5 (9-10 year olds) the lessons gradually advance from description and observation to thoughtful consideration, observant thinking, generalization and abstraction in the upper grades.

For example, the French Revolution is presented as a conflict of ideas and forces. Individual biographies with which the pupils can identify illustrate this process. Similarly, hearing about the often tragic life and struggles of an explorer or inventor makes them realize that exploration of the laws of nature, and technical inventions, are the fruits of human thought.

This communication of pictorial-descriptive experience is meant to avert a danger threatening in particular those at or after the age of puberty: the danger that they cannot relate what they learn about nature or the life of humanity to their own existence. Helping them to grow gradually into the natural and social world into which they were born is intended to foster their growth to mental and psychological maturity, to assist them in finding their identity.

Last but not least, stories provide material for verbal or written recapitulation. This promotes an ability to speak clearly, to remember experiences and express them coherently. Furthermore, the children assimilate forms of expression. Unconsciously they recreate particular turns of phrase or modes of formulation, thus enriching their vocabulary and acquiring a feeling for language, rhythm, and melodic pattern. Without such preparation the poetry block period in Grade 10 would be dry and barren.

While story-telling prepares for subject lessons, the fairy tales told in the first school year may be said to prepare for the whole of life. Each fairy tale describes how goodwill overcomes all hazards and leads to the goal. The wisdom of fairy tales stems from their belief in the power of goodwill and in the forces in life helping those who pursue their path with such a will. With them the children can identify. The teacher recounting these archetypes of human destiny - speaking without a script so that he can watch the children's reaction -, becomes himself the hero who surmounts so many obstacles, who saves or is saved. He is thus a living proof of the intrinsic truth of the tales. In his years with a class the teacher often has opportunities of observing how deeply these pictures sink into the children's minds and engender a healthy inner attitude to life.

In all fairy tales the imagery speaks of the spiritual past and future of the human soul. They do not describe individual fates but the changes the soul undergoes on the way to conscious, free humanity. These changes are subject to spiritual laws and order and are common to all men. The themes of fairy tales - ordeals and the successful overcoming of them, expulsion and marriage, the casting of spells and deliverance from them - derive from a knowledge of death and resurrection, which the tales implant in the children's spirit. These archetypal spiritual images supply the child with an arsenal of profound psychological importance for his entire life. Complete lack of them impoverishes and desiccates the soul with the result that, owing to psycho-physical interaction, physical disturbances occur.

Waldorf pedagogy is based on the conviction that the original versions of fairy tales, which reveal their inner logic, awaken soul and body building forces because they generate in the children's subconscious images of the sense and purpose of human life which can later develop into creative imagination, cognitive powers and social abilities. Moreover, the ties created between the pupils through the daily listening of the whole class counterbalance the egoism inevitably fostered by demands for achievement. This applies not only to fairy tales but to any story-telling that provides shared imaginative experiences.

Ursula Schulz

2.2.3 *The social aspect of a class community*

The Waldorf School curriculum is built on classes of children of the same age, in which the individual talents of all pupils are to be fostered in accordance with the specific needs and abilities of their age. This rules out any repetition of grades. It may be asked how a class teacher can lead a class of pupils with widely differing gifts through eight years without disadvantaging the bright ones or, no less important, the weaker ones. The answer is that the curriculum enables him to consider not merely the pupils' intellectual powers but to provide equal social, practical-artistic and intellectual stimulation which will promote mutual perception, recognition and consideration.

When evaluation is not based on achievement marks, which encourage egoism, but quite evidently on the intention to further every pupil, a similar attitude spreads within the class. Furthermore, the differing aptitudes promote each other, establishing a certain balance of the whole. This interplay of varying gifts is enhanced if the teacher utilizes the temperamental disposition of the children in the learning process.

An instrument for doing so is the old concept of the four temperaments, adapted for teachers' use by Rudolf Steiner. In the first lesson, when the children copy into their exercise books the archetype of all forms, a straight and a curved line which the teacher has drawn on the blackboard, they immediately reveal to him the four basic temperaments and their intermediate variations. One child draws his lines without hesitation in the centre of the page and has soon finished - the sign of a sanguine temperament. Others need much more time, and some draw figures so big that they spill over the edges of the paper like rising dough - they are the phlegmatic ones. A melancholic tackles the task hesitatingly, almost fearfully, worrying whether he is doing it correctly. His lines are thin and delicate, sometimes squeezed right into a corner of the page. By contrast, a real choleric puts them firmly and unmistakably in the centre, with such force that they show through on the pages underneath. Of course, not every child shows his temperament so clearly, but on the whole it is soon possible to discover which of the four basic ones predominates.

One of the teacher's artifices is to seat children with related temperaments together in groups. Thus they experience their neighbour's one-sidedness, and this unconsciously affects their own. For example, the excitable sanguines at first merely intensify each other's restlessness. But they soon get tired of it and gradually calm down. A melancholic may be distracted from his own preoccupations by his neighbour's worrying and thus come out of his isolation a little. Indifferent phlegmatics get bored among their own kind and begin to take more interest in the life of the class. The most salient case is the choleric who insists on having his own way in everything. Coming up against equally determined resistance from his classmates may teach him some degree of self-restraint. In the lessons the teacher tries to appeal now to one, then to another temperament, and this becomes an important factor in enhancing his self-control and his differentiated treatment of the class. The aim of this procedure is to harmonize the children's natures by helping them to overcome their one-sidedness. For instance, an energetic, perhaps even somewhat violent choleric misses whole areas of experience because he rushes blindly past all that is delicate. But if he gains something of the lightheartedness of sanguines, the preserving care of phlegmatics or the depth of feeling and dedication often found in melancholics, if he learns thereby to control his power, then his energy and enthusiasm can become fruitful both for himself and for his environment.

At first a temperament must be accepted in all its manifestations, but left to itself its one-sidedness bars the gate to experience of the world. A class community in which every member can develop on equal terms with the others and can compare himself with them from the decisive age of school entry to puberty, is very conducive to achieving a healthy balance. The following outline of the development of two pupils may serve as an example.

Anneliese, a red-cheeked, impulsive daughter of a miner, had a strong lisp. She had great difficulty in drawing the shapes of letters on a large sheet of paper, and for two years she hardly dared to speak. It was not until the third school year that she learnt to write words legibly, and not until the fifth that she succeeded in laboriously reading sentences. In mathematics she had to make a great effort to achieve the required level. In the first few years she expressed with gestures what she could not utter in coherent sentences. But she followed the stories with understanding, and through speaking in chorus and role-playing she gradually gained more confidence. Her gaiety and helpfulness in games and rambles made her popular with her classmates. Her colour compositions in watercolours and her wax models were above average. In a conventional primary school Anneliese would most probably have had to repeat the second grade, perhaps also another one. But since there is no repetition of grades at the Hibernia School, she and her parents did not need to worry on that score. One of the contributory causes of her slow development was a specific speech barrier due to a lack of practice in speech at home. The obviously existing passive speech competence lacked the active component. Free from pressure to achieve a defined level in the first few years of school, and encouraged by gradually rising demands appropriate to her capabilities as well as by the undisturbed process of growing into the class community, the girl was able to reach an adequate level of achievement in all school subjects by the 6th school year.

Christian, a very bright boy with a stimulating home background, very quickly learnt to write, read and calculate. But he was bored by speaking exercises, although his poor enunciation and his loquaciousness called for deliberate speech training. Only when he was allowed to recite a poem or a piece of prose he had had to learn by heart did he take any trouble. The class teacher advised his parents to let him have music lessons as an artistic stimulation. Christian learnt to play the violin and became one of the leading violinists in a class where 16 other children played a stringed instrument and another 10 a wind instrument, such as the recorder, trumpet, or clarinet. In the course of the eight years Christian also acquired social skills. Through living together with intellectually less gifted children, such as Anneliese and others whose artistic skills, in many cases superior to his own, he admired, he learnt to accept them. From the fifth grade onwards he gladly took on the leadership in group tasks, and Anneliese unabashedly joined him, as she did later in written work. In the seventh and eighth grades he frequently arrived at the School some fifteen minutes before the lessons started in order to give help to certain pupils. With encouragement from the teacher, this voluntary commitment on the part of Christian, and Anneliese's willingness to accept help, developed over the long years they spent together as members of the class community.

At the end of each school year pupils receive reports (1) on their development and achievements. These reports are primarily meant for the parents, but they also contain so-called "report-maxims" - epigrams or short verses, often composed by the teacher with no claim to poetic perfection to fit each pupil's personality and with the intention of giving him a stimulus for the new school year. He then recites his maxim once a week. This concentration by the teacher on the pupil's individuality can create a relationship between them that extends far beyond the lessons.

After the eighth school year the class teacher hands his pupils over to a class counsellor, and their further education is provided by specialist teachers. However, the class teacher has the possibility of remaining in contact with the pupils right to the end of their schooling. He may occasionally help them or their teachers with advice based on his intimate knowledge of "his" pupils.

Rosemarie Bütow and Albrecht Ziegert

## 2.2.4 *Parents' involvement*

When parents enrol their children in the Hibernia School, they learn that they are expected to cooperate. Their children should not be left to make their way through school alone but should be given a home education which is on similar lines. Special forms of initiating and maintaining a relationship with the parents have been developed.

At least three times a year the parents of a class are invited to a parents' meeting. The class teacher, the school doctor and the specialist teachers (of languages, music, eurhythmy, needlework, modelling, woodwork and gardening) explain their methods and procedures by describing details of their lessons from the perspective of Rudolf Steiner's "Study of Man". In the course of time, questions and answers lead to a deeper understanding. Sometimes working groups are set up in which educational problems are discussed on the basis of Steiner's writings.

Wherever possible a class teacher pays several visits to his pupils' homes. This gives him an impression not only of the family situation but also of the fathers' and mothers' occupational and social activities. Such opportunities widen the teacher's horizon and enable him to relate his educational work more closely to contemporary conditions, an essential point in the Waldorf School conception.

Once a year the parents are invited to an afternoon party. In the decorated hall the children present examples of their work; they perform pieces of music, act short plays, or recite poems individually or in chorus (the older ones also in English and Russian, the two foreign languages taught at the School). Coffee and cakes are served, conversations start, and people get to know each other.

In the winter term the specialist teachers arrange courses and working groups for the parents in eurhythmy, use of language, painting, woodwork, copperwork, etc. It can be of immense help for the children to see that their parents enter into such new learning processes often with the greatest of pleasure. The following example will serve as an illustration of this.

In the first three years of school the children learn English and Russian entirely by repeating what the teacher says or by speaking together with him. Without learning individual words and grammatical concepts by heart, they absorb the foreign language through songs, verses, puzzles or games. As it is important that the parents should become aware of their children's powers of imitation, the teacher will occasionally invite them on a public holiday to join him and the children in practising singing and dancing games. The parents then see how quickly and unselfconsciously the children join in, whereas they themselves have to make a conscious effort and are much more inhibited. Those who have a large house or garden are sometimes stimulated by such an afternoon's activities to arrange something similar for their own children and for others who do not have the facilities at home. They organize games, do handicraft work with them or read to them.

Thus the parents of a class grow together into an educational working community which spreads all over the School and turns it into a place of communal cultural and social life.

Some parents are particularly interested in talking to new parents who wish to enrol their children. They tell them about the School community and their own experiences with the educational activities that go on. When the child has been accepted they also take over the negotiations about the required financial contribution, which must be related to the parents' income.

Activities of this kind lead to membership in the Parents' Advisory Committee, the Parents' Association and the Board of the School Association, all of which perform a definite function in the School as a whole.

Groups are also formed to organize the major school festivals. The summer festival, held just before the main holidays start, and the annual Christmas bazaar would be unthinkable without the parents' active participation. The summer festival is a riot of activity. The youngest children have sack races, egg and spoon races, races on stilts; the 7th grade puts on a circus performance, with acrobats thoroughly trained in the gymnastics lessons and imaginatively decked out animals who are put through their paces; shouts and shrieks mark the spot where Grade 8 is operating a ghost train which they have built themselves in many hours of concentrated work. Parents and teachers in costume compete in volleyball matches and obstacle races.

The Christmas season is equally busy and colourful. During Advent candles are lit every morning; there are songs and religious plays, and in the evenings teachers, parents and the older pupils make dolls, soft toy animals, children's clothing, pottery, bookbindings, wooden toys, calendars and Christmas decorations for the bazaar.

Besides these two main events, there are dramatic performances, sometimes in foreign languages. The principal occasions are the plays staged at the end of Grades 8 and 10. From time to time parents and others are invited to the monthly or quarterly festivals in which the children display what they have learnt in music and eurhythmy, recitation, foreign languages or gymnastics.

The concerts held at least once a year are of particular

interest to the parents, many of whom make considerable sacrifices to let their children take music lessons. The School assists them by lending instruments and arranging group lessons from specialist teachers. Musicians who are friends of the School give regular concerts in the festival hall.

All these activities attract family friends and relations, and in particular ex-pupils who often travel long distances to meet their old classmates or to show their friends what goes on in "their" School.

In the autumn a weekend seminar is held, if possible in combination with an Open Day. The visitors are taken round the School. In the classroom samples of the pupils' work are exhibited, such as block period diaries, needlework, geometric drawings, wood and clay models, paintings and drawings, objects from the workshops. Parents, pupils in the upper grades and teachers then meet in art or craft courses or discussion groups where they consider the concept of the School from their various viewpoints and experiences and cooperate in defining its objectives. Many an adult finds in such a weekend of painting or modelling relief from the stress of everyday life, a revitalization he would like to experience again and again. The teaching staff, too, draw fresh inspiration from these encounters and broaden their horizons.

Albrecht Ziegert

## 2.3 The structure of practical education in Grades 1-8 or 9

### 2.3.1 *Principal issues in practical education*

It is a special characteristic of the Hibernia School that from the very outset the pupils do practical handicraft work prior to any occupational specialization. Four aspects determine the Hibernia School's concept of practical education:

1) How can children's urge to be active, to move, to do something, in short their *urge for activity*, be utilized by the School?

2) How can the productive imagination the children display in their games be transformed into conscious and controlled creativity?

3) How can the initiative and readiness to learn shown by a child at play be harnessed so that it produces a sound attitude to work in adulthood?

4) How can the child be trained in bodily skills, especially in the use of his hands, so as to promote a general "grasp" which corresponds to the stages of his development?

Figure 5 shows how the handicraft curriculum for Grades 1-6 is designed to develop and refine the children's ability on the first lap of this journey. In the needlework lessons, for instance, they first learn to knit and crochet (2.3.2 and 2.3.3), then to embroider, sew and knot so as to have practice in the skilful use of fingers and tools.

These activities are still largely of a rhythmic and artistic nature. They form part of an overall "movement education" which includes running in patterns in the main lessons, as well as eurhythmy and a variety of games.

2.3.2 *Knitting lessons in Grade 1*

It needs a real effort to visualize the complicated process involved in knitting: a theoretically endless thread must be looped and relooped, fastened on the right, on the left, at the top and at the bottom so as to produce a meshed fabric which could be undone by merely pulling on the thread. How can boys and girls in Grade 1 learn to accomplish this ambitious task?

They look at their hands, and each finger gets a name, such as "the little rascal", or "the thick thumb". Then the thread has to be wound correctly around the fingers of the left hand, a process which takes a long time to learn. Once it is mastered, the knitting needles are introduced. Now all ten fingers are fully occupied, each having its own job to perform. A song describing the process helps to remember every detail. It is not easy for young children to acquire this manual skill, the theoretical aspects of which are quite beyond their mental grasp. But they experience with pride how something is being created by their own hands - something that grows bigger and bigger and would grow to the end of the world if they did not stop working at it. Thus at the beginning they always want to do something big, a scarf or a dress. But they soon see how much hard work and concentration is required to finish even a small item, such as a cover for a recorder. Gradually the dexterity, the "fingertip feel" the children's hands have acquired in the process, is passed on to their heads, laying the foundation for fluid thinking. It may enable them in later life to

Handicraft Curriculum for Grades 1-6

| Age | Grade | 2-hour lessons throughout the school year ||| General Knowledge Block Period combined with handicraft practice |
| | | Needlework | Modelling/Carving | Gardening | |
| 12 | 6 | Sewing and stuffing of dolls and toy animals | Rasping of free and purpose-tied forms | Work providing experience of the annual vegetation cycle | Forestry block period in the School cottage, 2 weeks full time |
| 11 | 5 | Knitting with 5 needles (socks) | Handcarving, clay modelling | " | |
| 10 | 4 | Embroidery (cross-stitch) | Wax modelling in main lessons | | |
| 9 | 3 | Embroidery | " | | Agriculture and bread baking periods, house-building period, approx. 4 weeks each in main lessons |
| 8 | 2 | Crocheting | " | | |
| 7 | 1 | Knitting | " | | |

FIGURE 5

hold on to the thread of events, to connect one experience with another and so to give a meaning to whatever happens.

Hildegard Rist

### 2.3.3 *Needlework in the early grades*

In Grade 2 crocheting is practised. While knitting makes equal demands on both hands, the stress in crocheting is chiefly on one hand. Being an easier technique it does not rivet the children's attention entirely to the technical process and leaves more scope for artistic experiences.

In Grade 3, at nine years of age, the children undergo a change of consciousness. Until then they felt at one with the world, bound up with their environment; now they begin to confront the world in a more wakeful, concrete, objective manner. That means more detachment and the first signs of critical awareness.

In needlework lessons the children are therefore given tasks which demand greater consciousness, and hence distance from their manual activity and from the object they are making. One such simple task is to embroider a napkin case with a pattern combining aesthetic and functional aspects. Along the outer edges, where the case is touched when it is opened, darker colours are used which do not get dirty so easily. Towards the centre they are shaded off into lighter, more delicate colours. Work of this kind in Grades 3 and 4 draws the children's attention to the artistic designing of form, colour and structure, while manual skill is also practised.

### 2.3.4 *Baking bread in Grade 3*

The children wash their hands, put on aprons and march into the school kitchen where the cook has already prepared the yeast and set out big basins with flour and sugar. They are very excited because they are going to bake "Sunday bread". Each child fetches his ration of floor and sugar, and yeast and flakes of butter are distributed. Covering these neatly with the powdery flour needs care and concentration. Then the kneading starts, easy work which the children love doing, though some who did not sprinkle enough flour on the dough soon have it sticking all over their hands and have to rub it off with flour before they can continue. Others, comparing their piece of dough with those of their neighbours, notice that it is dry and cracking. They have to pour some milk carefully into a hollow and re-knead the dough. When finally all the dough has been sufficiently kneaded and rolled, it must be left to rest and rise. It is covered with a clean kitchen towel because it likes warmth and must be protected from draught. While the children clean up the kitchen they wonder what is happening there under those towels, what peculiar process it may be that is at the same time a rest and a rising. When they take the towels off they are amazed at the transformation that has taken place. Then they knead the dough again, form and decorate the loaves and put them on a baking sheet, not too close together because they will rise again.

The block lesson on baking is preceded by one on farming. The children plough their own little strip of land with a small plough which eight of them pull and one guides. Then come harrowing and hand-sowing. During the next few months the children often go to the school garden to see how their grain is growing. Then comes the harvesting, and finally the grain is ground in a coffee grinder.

In this way the children learn by doing how great a number of things have to be considered, prepared and accomplished in order to produce the loaf of bread for their sandwiches.

Rosemarie Bütow

2.3.5 *False romanticism in education?*

It may be asked whether in an era of mechanical farming and bread factories it is justified to let the children make bread in this traditional way and to talk to them about hand-sowing, sickles and wind- or water-mills. The answer is that the appropriate time for these block periods is Grade 3, when the children begin to face the world more consciously and are ready to turn their interest and feeling to a more complex economic process, comprising several operational phases, which they can execute themselves. This is possible only at its original level.

Through doing all operations involved, they learn not merely to understand the entire process cognitively and passively. They experience it at work. Such understanding gives them the confidence that they will be able gradually to grasp other things in the seemingly confusing diversity of their environment. This is an important help for further learning. Lack of understanding and of learning motivation are often due to the abstract and incomprehensible nature of the learning content. Such failures frighten children. That is why the Waldorf School endeavours to provide them with experiences which will enhance their self-confidence. If all the enthusiasm nine-year olds are capable of is directed into an activity showing them how a daily needed commodity, such as bread, is produced by utilizing the gifts of nature, their active interest is aroused in a part of their environment to which they had until then given no thought. And this active interest is essential for an understanding of the economic, social, technological, nutritional and other problems they will learn about in the course of their schooling.

### 2.3.6 *Knitting a pair of socks in Grade 5 needlework lessons*

The knitting practice the pupils have acquired in Grade 1 is now put to use in knitting a pair of socks to fit their own feet. To accomplish this, undivided attention and precise observation are needed, for the knitting must constantly be adjusted to the shape and size of the foot by increasing and decreasing, continuing with a certain part of the sock and then joining it up with the other parts. The heel must enclose the foot firmly but comfortably. Doing the middle part is comparatively easy, and this stretch of plain knitting is often accompanied by gay conversation. But the toes are tricky again. Over and over again the pupils have to try on the piece they have already done to make sure that it fits exactly. Never before have they looked at their feet so closely. Looking at their classmates' feet they also notice that there are many different shapes. Some are broad, some pointed, some oval. To produce a sock that will fit snugly across the toes they must also be able to visualize just how each stitch cast on or off will change the whole shape. And all of this has to be repeated for the second sock.

This is a new level of practical learning and craftsmanship, where the form of the product to be made must be carefully matched to a natural object and constantly checked against it. A preparation for the necessary perception and differentiation of individual body formations had been the Grade 4 block period "Study of the Human Body", in which the children were made aware of the differences of human heads, rumps and limbs, when they drew or described them in their block period diaries and compared them with those of animals. The difference between the structure of, say, a lion's paw or a cow's hoof and a human foot thus became very clear to them. The concepts acquired in this way are consolidated by the precise observation and reproduction of the shape of their own feet. Together with the power of observation which has been trained in the practical work, these deepened concepts are to serve as a foundation for a knowledge of human nature and of the self.

Frieda Beck

## 2.3.7 *Clay modelling and wood carving in Grade 5*

Each child is given a lump of clay of a size it can enclose with its two hands. This lump has to be kneaded carefully by rolling it repeatedly on the table with the palms and balls of the thumbs and by gathering it up again into a lump with the whole hands. While they are doing this the pupils are told about the origin of the clay, the various kinds of clay, and how to make it durable. The kneaded clay is then made into a ball by surrounding it with both hands and pressing from all sides towards the centre. With fingertips pressed together a small dent is made all round the ball until it begins to divide in two. Now the whole hands work around the form until it becomes a twin-domed structure. How can this be turned into a likeness of a living creature?

The task involves recognising the posture of an awakening, sniffing, sitting, crouching, slinking, running or butting animal, internalizing it and translating it into clay. Where fine detail is concerned, the fingertips do most of the work; convex curves are made with the whole palm, concave ones more with the ball of the thumb and with the fingertips. Among the fingers the thumb performs the special function of pushing and pressing. During their work the pupils frequently turn the figure around or walk round it, following each curve and each dent with their own bodies. Soon the hands learn to do much of what the whole body had to do at the beginning: groping around the form they can convey a feeling of what is happening at the back or in a hollow. Thus the hands are both reconnoiterers sensing out the processes of interaction between material and form, and tools transferring what has been felt into the material. At all times the hands' actions express an inner activity, the feeling and movement of the entire individual.

With their hands thus trained, the children can start carving with a sharp knife. The first piece they work on is held in the hand. A small piece of lime tree branch, its circumference just big enough to be enclosed by the hand, and a knife for carving are all that is needed at this stage. Seeing the children sitting on their stools, bent over their work in silent concentration, one feels that this is the right kind of activity for their age. They can follow with their eyes what their hands are doing, and they are still closely connected with the workpiece through holding it in their hands. Guiding the sharp knife requires more concentration than all the tools they have used before, and at the beginning there are lots of bleeding fingers. But after a few lessons most children carve with surprising assurance. First they carve the top end of their piece into a nice round dome. Then each child has to decide what he wants to make. It should be a rounded form representing, if possible, something living. In due course the twin-domed ball becomes a hedgehog, an elephant, a polar bear, a rabbit or even a calf. Some get no further than a ball or an egg. Others who have got a thin branch carve an upright human figure. It takes many hours for the children to see clearly to which shape their piece of wood lends itself best. Some lose patience and have to be encouraged to continue, others are fully immersed in their work and make their own decisions. Only a few ask what they should carve. In such cases the whole class gathers around to find out the intrinsic possibilities of the piece of wood concerned.

In the sixth school year the pupils start to use the vice on the bench. When the thing they are making is no longer held in the hand but by the vice, they are a little more detached from it and have both hands free for the tools. The small knife is replaced by a bigger rasp, and soon after by a gouge. Not only the hands, but the whole body is now involved. In Grades 7 and 8 the children practise carving with the gouge. Manipulating it requires fingertip control, because it works into the material and has to be consciously guided. Each cut can be watched throughout, which was not possible in rasping. The curriculum thus follows, in a manner suited to the pupils' developmental phase, the traditional unity of art and craft which existed up to the era of industrial production.

Maria Garbe

2.3.8 *Dolls and soft toy animals in Grade 6 needlework lessons*

In Grade 5 the children's own feet served as a pattern when they were making socks, but the more highly developed power of abstraction in the sixth year of school makes it possible for them to design their own patterns. In the nature study lessons of Grade 5 the specific shapes of animal bodies were discussed, and the human body in its various functions was presented as a selected summary of the diversity existing in the animal kingdom. The fact that the shapes and movements of animals are determined by specific functions - in the case of the dog, for instance, by his dominant sense of smell - occupies the children's minds intensely. They are deeply impressed by the realization that all these dispositions and capabilities are present in man in a harmonious combination and can be used as he wishes. Now they are required to convert these inner images into visible forms.

First the boys and girls sew a doll. Each child sits in front of a huge heap of featherlight, fluffy wool, pressing it little by little into a firm ball. A suitable piece of knit wear fabric is then pulled over the ball, tightened and tied up at the bottom to become a doll's head, with a little wool hanging out for the neck. The finer shaping of the head is done by tying threads. Each head turns out differently - big or small, round or oval. Body and limbs are roughly made from the remnants of material and are indicated by the form of clothing.

Next comes the sewing and stuffing of animals. Each child chooses an animal. To reproduce it in a simplified form, its main characteristics must be brought to mind: soft mouth, long or short neck, etc. Most children decide quickly which animal they want to make, and draw a pattern of it in the chosen size and posture. They also have to think of the technical aspects, such as the materials needed, and how to make the finished animal stand up. The pattern is first cut out of paper, then transferred to the fabric and sewn together. The extremely varied and often comical results, particularly when the fabric is being stuffed, are greeted by the class with laughter, jeering or admiration, as the case may be. But since everyone has himself experienced the difficulties involved, and some bright children who had underestimated the task have made a mess of it, they readily accept other less successful creations and take an unenvious delight in especially good ones.

Frieda Beck

2.3.9 *Gardening instruction in Grades 5-9*

Dotted around the School compound are flower beds, vegetable patches, shrubs, a large variety of trees, a hothouse and a tree nursery, presenting the pupils with different gardening tasks throughout the year.

In Grades 5 and 6 they have two gardening lessons per week so that they can experience the annual cycle of nature in their own activities. From Grade 7 onwards they have a three week block period in which to accomplish more extensive jobs. After Easter, at the beginning of the annual cycle, the 11 year olds first start working in the garden. To most of the children living in the Ruhr area with its predominantly urban and industrial environment, planting and harvesting is something entirely new. They have been looking forward to it with keen anticipation. In the first few lessons they get to know the tools. The shape and function of a pickaxe, hoe, spade, shovel, four-pronged fork, etc. are first expressed by gestures and hand movements until the children come to understand how to handle them functionally. Carrying the implements correctly so as to avoid injuring others - metal pointing downwards, not across the shoulder - is part of this exercise. Good habits acquired from the start benefit future work.

One of the first jobs is digging and levelling a patch, making seed rows and putting seeds in. It is a rewarding experience for boys and girls to see how small seeds develop in the course of the year into huge sunflowers, which are then cut to decorate the hall at festivals. All activities are demonstrated rather than explained, for at that age children still imitate half in play. They adopt as a matter of course all the unaccustomed postures, such as squatting, kneeling, bending, digging, because they see that these are necessary.

In their activities the pupils get to know what are the right conditions for plants. If the soil is too dry, it must be watered, otherwise the plant will wilt. Young plants must be protected from too much sun. Weeds must be pulled out because they would overpower the cultivated plants. Some plants are studied in more detail. Without naming them, the teacher describes their major characteristics, for instance the differing shape of their leaves from ground level to flower base. The overall form of the plant determines the colour of its flowers. A blue flowering plant can vary within the spectral range of blue; it may produce white and pink flowers, but never yellow or orange ones. The conditions for a plant to grow can also be deduced from certain characteristics. The name of the plant is not revealed until most of the children have guessed which one has been described. This method teaches careful observation and recognition.

In rainy weather drawings of individual plants are done

from memory. It has to be an accurate reproduction conveying something of the essence of the plant. On such days there are also detailed talks about the life of the soil - worms and ants, beetles and fungi, humus, sun, wind and rain. In this way the children gain access to an infinitely rich world into which they can penetrate ever more deeply throughout their lives.

In Grade 7 the pupils are capable of more intensive and differentiated work. In groups of some 15 boys and girls they do two hours of gardening in the afternoon for three weeks. With the activities they have already learnt thus connected from one day to the next, the children come to understand their correct sequence. At a daily introductory discussion the individual jobs are allocated according to the time of year and the situation in the garden. For instance, on a day in late May ornamental grasses have to be spread out, tall hollyhocks must be tied up to prevent their being broken by the wind, withered wallflowers must be removed to make room for summer flowers, artichokes kept in the hothouse during the winter must be replanted now or never. Although the children are familiar with all the manual techniques involved, they must practise them with constant care and adapt them to the job in hand. The group planting the sprouting artichokes, for example, must decide at what distance to set the plants. Memories of the size the artichokes reached the year before, and of how their spines made it difficult to break up the soil round them, lead to the decision to plant them 1 m apart. Another group cutting back shrubs wonders whether they will ever bloom again if they are cut so drastically. After all, it is their nature to bear fruit and produce seeds. The pupils have to find a balance between cutting down so far that the plant will die, and cutting back far enough to concentrate the shrubs' strength for growth so that they will grow and flower again profusely. Once the pupils have understood this principle, they may later recognize it as a general law of life.

When the various jobs have reached a point where an interruption will cause no harm, pupils and teacher get together to discuss what has been done. This review of the work accomplished and of the jobs still to be done links one day to the next. In Grade 7 the pupils' eagerness to continue with the work they have started far outweighs their interest in the purpose and necessity of gardening techniques. While they experience the logical relationship between their activities and the living conditions of the plants, they do not give much thought to it. For this very reason they internalize the fact that gardening work is governed by a natural process which allows no interruption and demands that all actions be integrated with it. While in the technical workshops the pupils experience planned working that must be exactly calculated in advance and executed accordingly, in gardening they are surrounded by living things obeying their own laws, and these laws must also determine the work process. Planning and preparation are still necessary, but the results are produced by sun, rain and wind.

In Grade 9 the gardening block periods usually take place in winter. The pupils are now expected to work more or less independently. The cutting back of trees and shrubs requires an understanding of their growth patterns and growth conditions, as well as a general knowledge of the various plant categories. Coniferous plants with their strictly geometrical shape, deciduous trees with their freely balanced tops and shrubs with their regular repetition of equal-sized branches are distinct types. The 150 varieties growing in the School compound offer many different examples of these three groups. The children work out their basic structural laws by means of repeated observation and drawings.

The fundamental knowledge acquired in this way enables the pupils to tackle the task of cutting out branches with some assurance. First they practise the technique of sawing under the teacher's guidance, then independently. The wound caused by the cut must be small, the branch must not tear off the surrounding bark, the weight of the branch and the force of its fall must be taken into consideration. The pupils experience their responsibility, their actions have finality. No sawn-off branch can be put back on the tree! So every tree and shrub is thoroughly examined before cutting, the saw is carefully held at the correct angle, and every cutting wound is properly dressed. Composting and other earth work, planting young trees and, in the season before Christmas, making fir wreaths for decoration are other winter jobs.

Throughout their gardening work the pupils experience how man is surrounded by constraints he has not created himself, but which he can use for his own purposes if he adjusts to them. An even more important outcome is an awareness of nature as a vast self-contained world whose diversity arises not from transparent causal-mechanical connections, as is the case with technical processes, but can be comprehended only through sympathetic observation, through an artistic mode of consideration. This approach lays the foundation for future true insight into nature. Especially in the Ruhr area, where the sparse remains of natural vegetation are constantly encroached upon by allotment gardens, the children should learn at an early age that nature must not be excessively exploited for man's own purposes, and that the ecology of the earth demands certain sacrifices. This sensitivity towards the needs of living things may later be transferred to humans. It may assist the pupils in their kindergarten or hospital training to render selfless help even if it cannot bring about any fundamental improvement, and to become active in a wider social context.

Rudolf Krause

## 2.3.10 *Forestry work in Grade 7*

To give the 12 year olds an outlet for their active interest in nature, a period of practical learning in the forest has been instituted. For two weeks the children live together with their class teacher and the crafts or gardening teacher in an isolated area of the forest, working with the forester and his assistants. The forester talks to them about the landscape, the game they are likely to meet, the timber and how it is sown, planted, nursed and felled, the forest's importance for man, about air, water, economic value, and the birds that give man so much pleasure. Alle these matters are discussed either in the "lookout", the classroom of the forest-home, or preferably outdoors where the children can see and touch the things under discussion.

A lively and varied programme makes it easy for the children to live in this new world. At 9 a.m., after an early morning talk by the forester, the forestry workers take the children in small groups, armed with their work tools and a first aid box, to the various places of work in the forest. This walk, usually lasting 30-45 minutes, already provides many experiences of rivulets and brooks, rain and fog, sunshine and swamp, dense and open forest, and all sorts of small animals. The work is equally varied: digging up the ground for a tree nursery, transplanting saplings, weeding, planting out, clearing a thicket, cutting a fire-break, ridding young plantations of self-seeded rowan or birch saplings, removing the branches from larches, or clearing up the litter left behind by weekend hikers.

Out of pieces of disbranched, sawn and pointed wood something useful is made on the spot, such as a raised hide, a feeding trough, or a fence. All the groups participate in turn in this work, so that the finished piece is a result of their common effort. They particularly enjoy building a little cabin out of wood they have themselves helped to fell, to saw, transport and shape. They can hardly wait to move in as soon as it is finished. Thus they experience a complete production cycle from growth to felling and building. It is important that the work they are given should be not merely an exercise but something that is needed and would have had to be done by adults if they did not do it themselves.

Every day one group is detailed to cook, serve at table and do the other domestic chores. This also is important. The children realize that work must be done to ensure the well-being of each individual and of the community. Beds have to be made, potatoes have to be peeled, dishes have to be washed, floors have to be cleaned. After lunch they are tired enough to be glad of a nap before starting out again in the afternoon.

Each pupil writes down his impressions of the forestry period and illustrates his account with sketches and drawings. This consolidates his experiences. In the evenings and early mornings some of them are allowed to sit with the forester in the hide or to go stalking with him and so learn the art of keeping silent, watching, listening and observing.

There are, of course, also scouting games which involve creeping into bushes, climbing trees - and tearing one's clothes! A strenuous all-day trek makes the blood flow faster. In the mornings the pupils are awakened by songs or instrumental music. Sometimes the forester's horn calls them out in the middle of the night to a nocturnal outing. Another feature of the forestry period is charcoal burning, gay occasions when beech logs, fir cones, crackling aromatic fir twigs are burnt in the charcoal burner's hut to the accompaniment of songs, jokes and feasting on delicious, if sometimes slightly charred sausages.

Through the varied demands which the practical forestry period makes on the pupils' physique, their entire bodies are given intensive training in agility just before the pre-puberty growth spurt sets in.
Martin Zacharias

2.3.11 *The development phase of 13 and 14 year olds*

The forestry period prepares the pre-adolescents in a manner suited to their age for the block periods that follow:

gardening, basket-weaving, copperwork, work at the forge, locksmith's work, etc.

At that stage a child's mind gradually breaks out of the pictorial-sensory domain. His thinking becomes more abstract, enabling him to combine sensory perceptions and observations with his own thoughts. Quite obviously, work in the forest and the learning of simple basic craft skills provide experiences conducive to an inner development balanced between the sensory and the abstract realm.

The rhythm of the timetable (see Figure 6) is adapted to this development phase. It provides for daily manual activity over longer periods. Consequently, the school becomes a full-day school from Grade 7 onwards. Academic lessons calling for mental concentration are followed by artistic activities in which the pupils can give free rein to their creativity, such as music, eurhythmy, clay modelling and gymnastics, while the afternoon block periods of specialized art and crafts training in the workshops demand physical strength and stamina. For the duration of each block period the pupils have lunch together with the specialist teacher concerned. The class is divided into three groups.

### Typical Timetable for Grades 7 and 8

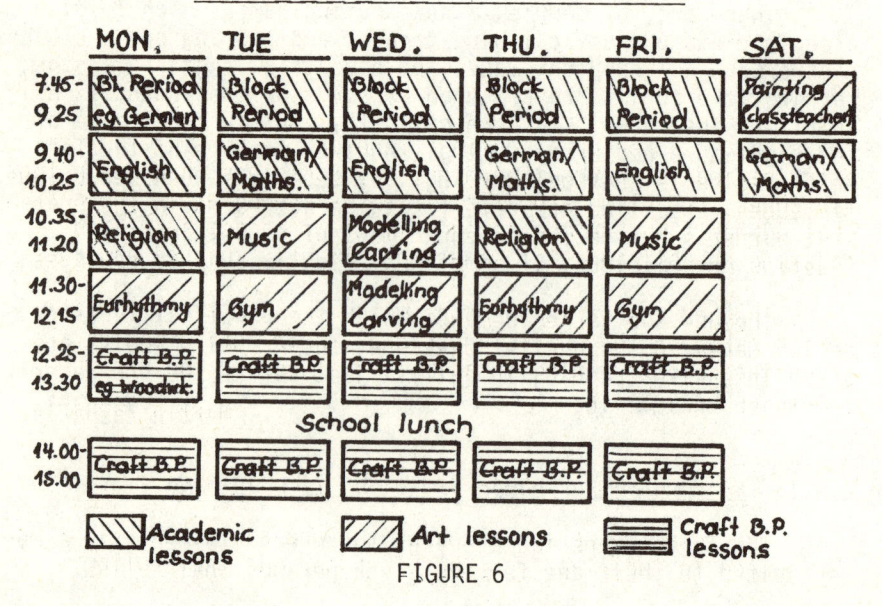

| | MON. | TUE. | WED. | THU. | FRI. | SAT. |
|---|---|---|---|---|---|---|
| 7.45–9.25 | Bl. Period eg German | Block Period | Block Period | Block Period | Block Period | Painting (classteacher) |
| 9.40–10.25 | English | German/Maths. | English | German/Maths. | English | German/Maths. |
| 10.35–11.20 | Religion | Music | Modelling Carving | Religion | Music | |
| 11.30–12.15 | Eurhythmy | Gym | Modelling Carving | Eurhythmy | Gym | |
| 12.25–13.30 | Craft B.P. eg Woodwk. | Craft B.P. | Craft B.P. | Craft B.P. | Craft B.P. | |
| | School lunch | | | | | |
| 14.00–15.00 | Craft B.P. | Craft B.P. | Craft B.P. | Craft B.P. | Craft B.P. | |

▨ Academic lessons    ▨ Art lessons    ▤ Craft B.P. lessons

FIGURE 6

The craft block period lessons are given during 21 weeks in Grade 7 and during 31 weeks in Grade 8. In the remaining weeks, when there is no afternoon crafts teaching, Grade 8 rehearses a play.

2.3.12 *Woodwork in Grades 7 and 8*

The first stage of specialized, accurate craft work begins with woodwork lessons in Grade 7, when the pupils are 13 to 14 years old. They start with chopping and sawing, i.e. the elementary handling of the splitting wedge, axe, hatchet, hacksaw and hammer to make firewood from pieces of tree trunk. Next, logs or branches are pieced together into a climbing frame or a log cabin, or a toy for the kindergarten. The way in which the children work with an axe or a saw is still very similar to what they did in the forestry period.

In the next two block periods they learn how to handle a scraper and a plane. These activities are already an approach to the acquisition of specialized skills. The pupils enter the age at which they lose the easy assurance of childhood and have to regain it through independent thought. The teacher will observe how at the beginning of each block period the pupils lack confidence in themselves because they have to think out and work out the processes involved. It helps everybody if each working process, each manual operation is first discussed and demonstrated by the teacher to the whole group, so that they can learn the necessary skills by imitation. This trains them in awareness of their own hands and of their potentialities.

One block period in the second semester of Grade 7 is devoted to work with the scraper. Round logs, some 8-10 cm in diameter, are split into half and the cut surface is then levelled off with the scraper. This requires a feel for the wood, its structure and grain. Next, a second level surface must be cut at right angles to the first. These half-logs are then cut to the required length, glued and nailed together to form a bird-table or a nesting-box.

Planing is taught in the first block period in Grade 8. Strength, patience, stamina and skill are needed to become familiar with the plane and to learn how to handle it. When a pupil has finally produced a bench or a flower-stand, he can proudly say that he has made it entirely by himself from a chunk of tree. This kind of work is still comparatively easy, because it only involves executing the various operations which the teacher has demonstrated and gaining experience and assurance through practice. Though some independent thinking is needed, the determining factor is still imitation.

When in the latter part of Grade 8 the pupils come back to the workshop for their second woodwork block period, they seem barely recognizable. They have changed physically, and even more markedly in the way they work. Most of them are no longer as quick and sure as they used to be in grasping what has to be done. They are less responsive, have greater difficulties, tend to be somewhat clumsy. Although most of them appear stronger, more conscious and independent, these apparent capabilities still have to be created and developed.

This is the period in which they learn to make wooden toys. It is so conceived as to give the pupils confidence in their ideas, plans and designs. The intention is to make them experience that their imagination combined with manual skill can produce successful results. Through this experience they will regain some assurance and self-confidence. At the age of puberty such reassurances are very important. They are stones building the bridge which leads from childhood to adulthood.

To promote functional thinking, movable toys are made. They should be robust and versatile, but not so finished in every detail as to leave no room for the imagination of the children who are to play with them. Many movement variations are feasible. The toys may have wheels so that the child can pull or push them, and in addition some part may move sideways or up and down. Such a combination is already part of the realm of mechanics.

The object of this work is to develop the pupils' inventiveness and ingenuity in tackling technical problems. They must, of course, be stimulated, their brains must be set in motion. This is becoming increasingly difficult because nowadays they are used to readymade things. But experience has shown that they suddenly begin to enjoy pondering over solutions, trying out, experimenting, fiddling. As in the preceding block periods, they do all the operations involved themselves, by hand, cutting the different parts of the toys out of raw wood, splitting, sawing, planing, grooving and notching them and fitting them together. Matching the parts accurately requires precision, and constructing systems of movement transmission demands exact understanding of the mechanical process.

Most pupils are full of ideas. They produce cranes, trucks with cranes or tractors, cars of all kinds, railways, steam-rollers, bulldozers, hammer-mills, etc., or nodding, climbing, rotating animals and skilful trapeze artists. Each toy has multiple motion. For instance, if a vehicle moves forward, something in or on it rises and falls, rings or strikes, rotates, nods or sways.

Those pupils who are keen on inventing must learn by experience whether their ideas are feasible. Their thinking is tested and corrected by feasibility. Others are too timid or incapable of developing ideas of their own. In such cases co-operation between workroom teacher and class teacher is of particular importance for stimulating unimaginative pupils in other subjects as well. A special kind of group work, where each pupil constructs his own toy entirely but is given suggestions by the other members of the group, is often helpful. Difficult operations are done jointly.

Martin Zacharias

## 2.3.13 *Basket-weaving in Grade 8*

In one of the art and craft block periods lasting three weeks, the Grade 8 pupils learn basket-weaving. A simple wastepaper basket whithout handles is to be made, without a template, so that throughout the long working process their full attention is focussed on its shape. This is determined by each pupil's temperament and inclination, i.e. by the way in which he masters the difficulties of the rather complicated three-stage process. In this respect the activity is an artistic one.

A basic shape fulfilling the functions of a wastepaper basket serves as a guide: It must stand firmly, have sufficient holding capacity and widen slightly towards the top. Possible variations are beaker shape or bell shape. Greatly deviating forms, such as bowl or trumpet shape, do not answer the purpose. Cylindrical shapes appeal to the tidy-minded but usually turn out to be more suitable for umbrella stands than for wastepaper baskets.

The material is less familiar to the pupils than is wood. Even after thorough soaking in water the willow rods measuring approximately 1.60 m in length remain tough and intractable. The tools used are pruning shears, short kitchen knives and awls. To make the basket bottom, ten 25-30 cm long pieces of osier are interlaced to form a cross and, starting from its square center, two full-length osiers are then twined spirally through this cross. Then holes have to be bored into the rim of this wicker plate at equal distances, and twenty long osiers pushed deep into the holes. This operation calls for determined use of force; the weaker pupils can compensate for the strength they lack by clever handling of the awl and greater willpower.

The next operation, bending the long and obstreperous osiers, which stick out chaotically from the plate, into a vertical position without breaking them is equally strenuous and very hard on the thumbs; the pupils need a good deal of self-control to continue working with their aching thumbs until the last osier is in position. Now the weaving starts. Two osiers have to be wound, in opposite direction, through the vertical ones. After each round they must be pressed down until the first frame is completed. When the second or third frame is done, a total of 600 or 900 winding operations have been performed. The basket is then finished off with a plaited osier rim.

This work requires much feel for the material, fingertip control and care. Attention wanders to and fro from weaving to forming and vice versa. In between the workpiece must be looked at with a critical eye to see whether it is taking the desired shape, and corrections have to be made where necessary. This rhythmic swinging of attention from detail to the whole and back to detail has a calming effect. Many an inhibition or tautness dissolves in this work. Far from boring the pupils, it tends to relax them once they have developed a certain working routine. Sometimes they spontaneously start to sing. Finishing the baskets at the top and bottom again requires mental concentration.

Basket-weaving is done in Grade 8 because at that age the pupils should have the necessary strength and skill. Besides, it seems to mirror the developmental stage of 14 year olds. Out of apparent chaos they create a harmonious form. Their handling of specific material, their dexterity, imagination and sustained concentration are developed. And the finished product is a practical article for everyday use.

Detlef Böhm and Georg Metzner

2.3.14 *Copperwork in Grades 8 and 9*

Copperwork in Grade 8 initiates the pupils into working with metal. Whereas in gardening and woodwork they were still in close touch with the growth and formation of their material, copper sheeting is a product of technical processes unknown to them. While the smooth, shining surface of the material may inspire them, its hardness corresponds to the factory-like working situation where each pupil has a definite place at a bench with a base plate of steel or hardwood in the vice and a two-faced hammer. The noise assaults their ears, the odour of red-hot metal irritates sensitive noses. All are given similar pieces of copper sheeting to work on, but each decides on the shape of the bowl he is going to make. First they take off the sharp edges of the sheet with a file. Then it is smoothed and toughened with light hammer strokes thinning it out towards the edges. The right hand swings the hammer, the left guides the sheet spirally across the base until the sheet takes on a three-dimensional form, concave on the inside and convex on the outside. When after further hammering on the inside the copper has become hard and firm, it is softened again by firing. This operation interrupts the monotonous and strenuous hammering. Although the pupils have to wield a relatively heavy hammer for hours on end, the need is not so much for strength as for regular rhythm requiring concentration, patience and stamina. Physically strong pupils often find this particularly difficult.

In the firing process the copper changes colour. Dotted lines of grey, yellow and red curve through the piece until it finally turns a dark glowing red. But when it is taken out of the fire it becomes a dull black. It must then be cooled in water to regain its original colour and softness. Now the hammering continues until a small bowl with a rim 1-2 cm high is created. The more regular the hammering, the more perfect the finished article.

In Grade 9 a different technique suitable for making larger vessels is taught. The pupils fetch from the store a copper sheet 1 x 2 m in size and 1 mm thick and cut it into squares. These are placed on a steel mould of the intended shape and are hammered around this mould. This technique requires a finer feel for the tool and the metal because the stroke must be placed not on but next to the spot where the sheet is to touch the mould, in order to allow for expansion of the metal. It takes hours of hammering, interrupted only by repeated firing, for the sheet to take on some shape. Many pupils find this slow progress tedious and laborious. They have to struggle hard to summon up the necessary patience. A high degree of precision in guiding the hammer and the workpiece is required in order to transform the copper sheet first into any number of bowls of increasing depth, and finally into a tall beaker, jar or vase. In the process the pupils learn many things. They must maintain a relaxed posture. The movement starts from the shoulders, but it is the wrists that do most of the work. The hammer must be held loosely so that it can spring back in the rhythm of the strokes. Each pupil must find his own rhythm; he must not try to speed up the process by use of force. He must acquire the experience that rhythm saves strength.

                                              Klaus Arndt

## 2.3.15 On handicraft work in Grades 7 and 8

The developmental psychology underlying this intermediate stage in art and craft activities has been described in section 2.3.11. In the four woodwork block periods, manual skill and correct handling of tools are practised on an elementary level (chopping of firewood, work with the scraper, with the plane, and manufacturing of mechanical wooden toys). The tasks and techniques are increasingly divided into two distinct components, a technical and an artistic one. Basket-weaving still holds an intermediate position between these two components: the basket should have a pleasant shape, while the practical problems involved in producing it require strength, dexterity and intelligence. The material is closer to the softer materials of the lower grades (wax, clay and wood) than to the harder ones of the upper grades (copper, iron, steel). The finished product does not yet need to conform to an exact norm. In copperwork the pupils handle metal for the first time and get practical experience of a typical metal transformation process. At the same time copper is suitable for artistic creation, because it is a relatively soft and attractive material. The technical and the artistic components are still combined.

## 2.3.16 Healthy movement education in gymnastics

A small child develops in and through movement. This fact is fully recognized in contemporary infant care. But when the child has learnt to walk and can move easily, obstacles created by our civilization (crowded living conditions, lack of playgrounds, traffic, etc.) may seriously hamper his further development. A counterbalance must be provided through conscious movement education. Waldorf education tries to do this by promoting a healthy desire for movement.

It has been found in gym lessons that children taught in this way differ distinctly from others. Recently a second fifth grade (Vb) has been introduced into the Hibernia School. These pupils had previously attended other schools. They are now practising rope-skipping with one of the two gym teachers. Many of them are doing this for the first time in their lives and are unable to coordinate the differing movements of hands and feet. The rope keeps catching on their legs. Similar difficulties arise in other exercises which require a coordination of diverse movements, such as horse-vaulting or balancing on the beam. In a balancing lesson it transpires that some 80% of these pupils have never practised balancing on a tree trunk, a beam or anything similar. Some of them learn to do it quickly, others are too fidgety to muster the necessary inner calmness and concentration. They keep losing their balance. Others again are so awkward through overweight that they cannot react swiftly enough with slight balancing movements. Generally, the very fidgety and the very heavy children have great difficulty in learning gymnastic skills.

Through observations such as these the gym teacher realizes how great is the present-day lack of movement training through climbing, long walks, leaping over ditches or brooks, walking on uneven surfaces, helping in farm and forest work, all of which used to be a matter of course in former times. The results are insufficient body control and constitutional defects. In addition, the motor system is damaged by television, wrong nutrition, arhythmic living habits, etc.

By contrast, Waldorf pupils learn to move skilfully, swiftly and alertly in the gym lessons of Grades 1 and 2, the so-called gym games played with the teacher in the school yard. In Grades 3 and 4 the emphasis is on free play with a variety of gymnastic equipment, in which the children exploit all the movement possibilities offered. If, moreover, the teacher succeeds in stimulating the children's imagination to transform the big box into a hill, the blue mats into water and the balancing beam into a narrow plank across a stream, they will engage in these exercises with all the playful seriousness and involvement of their age.

Whereas in the lower grades the main object is to familiarize the children with the natural movement sequences involved in walking and running, leaping, skipping, romping, climbing, balancing and swinging, the emphasis in the upper grades is on practising social conduct in all kinds of games, alongside the systematic learning of skill in individual gymnastic or sporting activities.

Besides, the children's and adolescents' motor systems are stimulated in the eurhythmy, music, practical and main lessons. This manifold appeal together with the balanced timetable rhythm has a healthy and harmonizing effect. Again and again it becomes obvious in the conferences that pupils' difficulties in gymnastics show themselves in a modified form in other subjects. In such cases therapeutic measures, e.g. curative eurhythmy, are discussed with the school doctor. The gym teacher then has the best opportunities to observe whether or not these measures are successful.

An attempt is made to design the gym lessons for all age groups in such a way that:

- natural movement sequences are harmonized and cultivated; there is no intention to train for individual top performances;
- attention is always paid to the age-relatedness of the exercises.

Wolfgang Peter

## 2.3.17 Eurhythmy (2) lessons at Hibernia School

To the accompaniment of a musical instrument, the class teacher leads the first grade into the big eurhythmy room. Inside he continues walking until the head of the procession meets the tail end. But the pupils do not yet form a circle. There are gaps, some children stand apart. The teacher works indirectly towards a circular form by invoking the sun, whose perfection the children immediately understand. They begin to take their direction from the invisible centre, to become aware of their neighbours as the whole circle contracts or widens by taking a few steps. It becomes a living and moving thing, expanding or narrowing without losing its form. This social experience occurs only when all the children are fully involved. If the contraction and expansion of the circle is accompanied by corresponding movements of the arms, it resembles a giant flower which opens when there is light and warmth and closes when there is cold and darkness. The whole body takes part in such rhythmic movement. What may later become power of concentration (condensation) or devotion (expansion), is here done by the children in play, in their enjoyment of creating changes, of alternating between two polarities.

Although at that age imitation predominates, the circle exercise is particularly apt to arouse an awareness of jointly

executed movements. It takes considerable time until all the
children learn to move in harmony.

Just as the sun was a motivating image, the lurching bear,
the swiftly tripping mouse, the hopping rabbit, the slow-moving
snail are used as inspiration for short or long, swift or slow
steps. Thus prepared the children can follow the music and walk
its rhythms forwards and backwards in distinctly differentiated
steps. Next the arms follow the melody up and down. This implies coordinating two different movements: meaningful representation of a musical sequence by vertical movement of the
arms, and simultaneous walking of its rhythms, i.e. simultaneous
vertical and horizontal movement. This translation of sound
into movement requires concentration and immediate reaction.
Increasingly complex variations of the exercise learnt through
the years further the ability to coordinate all kinds of movement.

In Grade 4 the children's perception of music can be further enhanced through the introduction of a special movement
for each note. This may first be practised with a major scale,
then with simple tunes. To make a melody visible, the arms
must be moved easily, in a free flowing movement arising out of
inner feeling, just as tones are produced in singing. The form
of the gesture is developed out of the movement for each note.
Executed by two partners, one moving like the reflection of the
other, it becomes a form that changes between receding from and
re-approaching an axis. The close cooperation with the partner,
needed to produce a symmetrical design, ought to be within the
ability range of Grade 4 pupils.

A Grade 6 or 7 already tries to perform short pieces of
music, such as a Mozart sonatina. Once or twice a week throughout a term the forms for the upper and lower parts are worked
out and the rhythms and gestures practised, until the pupils
can control their movements without having to think about each
individual one. The human body becomes itself an instrument.
Many apparently unmusical pupils have found access to music
through the necessity of listening to it intently in order to
hear when, for instance, a major scale changes into a minor one
and the movement has to be changed accordingly.

A piece of music alternating between rapid, powerful movements in a major scale and slow ones in a minor scale appeals
to fifteen year olds (Grade 9), whose psycho-physical development is full of contrasts between turbulent restlessness and
loneliness. If these unconscious moods can be lifted to the

level of imagination and translated into activity, they become objective and help the young individual on the way towards the self-knowledge he is striving for.

In the same manner eurhythmy expresses language. The specific form-giving values of consonants and the soul qualities of vowels are translated into characteristic movements. Through movement developed from the laws governing language and music, the pupil acquires a capacity for deeper understanding of both as he grows older. He experiences them, and at the same time he learns to be fully aware of his partner. Thus he expands his individual experience potential as well as his social abilities. The empathy needed to experience a piece of music or literature and give it visible expression teaches him to alternate between immersing himself in it and withdrawing from it, a kind of inner breathing. As a result, emotions deriving from his physical constitution, such as lethargy or restlessness, can be brought under control through eurhythmy. Such conscious control of his physically conditioned emotions will help the pupil to acquire greater assurance and independence.

Since eurhythmy develops overall motor ability consonant with the various levels of human consciousness, it is an important help in learning other movement patterns and skills required for practical work. In assisting the pupils to practise such skills with inner involvement instead of performing them mechanically, it enhances their ability for lifelong learning in this field. Owing to psycho-physical interaction, eurhythmy is also beneficial to physical health, especially of children. It is well known that one-sided mechanical movements may cause physical damage. In such cases curative eurhythmy, which makes selective use of the healing powers of eurhythmic movement involving the entire personality, is applied to good effect. Generally, eurhythmy is seen as a means of counterbalancing the mechanical movements, or the lack of movement in sedentary occupations, to which many pupils will later be exposed in their working lives.

2.4   Grades 9-10

2.4.1 *Psychological development in the adolescent phase*

Human development occurs in oscillation between polarities. One such distinct swing of the pendulum is the transition from

childhood to adolescence at the age of puberty. i.e. at 13 or
14. Physically this transformation shows itself in body growth.
In Grade 6 nearly all boys and girls are of similar size. Two
years later, in Grade 8, there are tall ones and squat ones,
slender ones and plump ones, sturdy ones and lanky ones.

Corresponding changes can be observed in the pupils' behaviour. A Grade 8 pupil wants to know the reason for his tasks
and their purpose. He wants to see that what he is asked to do
will be really useful. He feels a need for his work to fit him
into a meaningful social context. On no account does he want
to be stimulated by moods. He is no longer willing to do something simply because everybody else is doing it, and he queries
what he used to accept on authority. He wants to understand the
Why and the Wherefore.

However, in Grades 7 and 8 the adolescents still depend
to a large extent on being shown what to do by the teacher, and
on his judgment. In Grades 9 and 10 they should learn to work
more independently, in accordance with their growing maturity.
All lessons now have the common objective of letting the pupils
experience the impersonal nature of matter and its intrinsic
demands. Objective experiences should gradually replace the
teacher as a source of learning. Self-education thus takes the
place of education by others. Learning from experience, acting
with understanding, overcoming incidental difficulties, controlling personal disinclinations, accepting causal connections
- these are aptitudes for which the adolescent must lay the
basis at this stage of his development.

2.4.2 *Articulation and diversification of the curriculum*

That the curriculum of the Hibernia School is vertically
articulated throughout the school years is evident from the emphasis laid in every teacher's report on age-relatedness of the
educational provision. In Grades 9 and 10 the three curricular
areas, i.e. academic, artistic and practical education, are
also horizontally articulated to foster the entire development
of the adolescents in this age group. This articulation involves not only subject matter and timetabling, but also an increase and intensification of educational effectiveness through
the interaction of various disciplines. How it is achieved in
practice is described in detail in sections 2.4.12 (Drawing and
painting), 2.4.16 (Mathematics and surveying) and 2.4.19
(Dramatics).

The diversification of the curriculum is illustrated by sections 2.4.12 (Drawing and painting), 2.4.13 (Locksmith's work), 2.4.14 (Machine operation), 2.4.15 (Vocational studies), 2.4.16 (Mathematics and surveying), 2.4.17 (Toy making), 2.4.18 (Poetry) and 2.4.19 (Dramatics).

### 2.4.3 *Class community and change of direction*

In Grade 9, specialist teachers and a class counsellor take over from the class teacher, who had until then given all theoretical block period lessons. This change from authority based on emotional attachment to authority based on specialized knowledge supports the process of depersonalization.

The class community remains together as a unit up to completion of Grade 12, when the pupils either leave school to enter employment or continue studying in preparation for a semi-professional or professional career. In the preceding years the class has become a social community with many links and relationships, with stability and an inner life of its own, which fulfil important educational functions at this and subsequent stages. In particular it helps the adolescents to experience more consciously the psychological changes they and their classmates are undergoing, and to become more objective, less subjective in a social context. Moreover, the stability of the class community, together with the practice of mutual support, assists weak pupils in attaining the various learning goals, especially cognitive ones. (3)

The long-standing cooperation with parents is continued by the specialized teachers, as are joint activities such as dramatics, surveying excursions, class travel, concerts and festivals.

### 2.4.4 *Psychological development through practical activity*

The functional activity practised in handicraft lessons furthers the pupils' psychological development. It directs their vaguely felt need to acquire an identity into a concrete effort to become independent in their judgement, decision-making and acting. For this reason the basic technical courses, such as blacksmith's and locksmith's work, start in this period. They set objective standards and are, therefore, an indispensable help to the pupils in finding their identity. There can be no doubt as to whose fault it is if the steel burns up, the measurements are incorrect, the parts do not match. Such continuous tangible and irrefutable controls constitute an essential component of the conduct appropriate to this age group. Success and failure are necessary experiences. Step by step the pupils learn self-control. In overcoming difficulties and finally producing a finished object, they gain self-confirmation which is objectively warranted. Handicraft work is, therefore, obligatory for all pupils.

14-15 year olds show a marked interest in getting to know various crafts without as yet desiring to specialize. In the Hibernia School they learn 13 different crafts in block periods of three weeks each. The curriculum combines attention to psychological development with suitable sequencing of handicraft skill learning. First, versatile manual skill is practised, then from Grade 10 onwards these skills are refined and the pupils advance to specialized work. Direct experience of technical rationality furthers this psychological development. Otherwise the curriculum does not differ much from that of Grades 7 and 8.

### 2.4.5 *Character training through work with iron, copper and wood*

Work in the smithy shows most clearly that the learning of a craft develops not only manual skill but also character. As the time during which the iron is pliable enough to be shaped is very short, the worker must use his force energetically, almost explosively. There is no room for hesitation, deliberation or timid experimentation. Despite this spontaneity and swiftness of action the blacksmith develops great precision, and if he produces a work of art he has achieved something to be proud of because it had to be done at speed. Observing Grade 9 pupils who are working in the smithy for the first time, one realizes how far they still have to go to attain such skill. The energetic ones have to struggle with the form, and those giving a great deal of thought to the form find that the iron has got cold by the time they are ready. When eventually two beaters succeed in producing a piece of work within a few minutes, they have obviously learnt more than mere manual skill.

Copperwork requires other character traits. Transforming a flat piece of sheeting into a vessel by series after series of hammer blows while shifting it spirally across the mould must be a slow flowing process if the material is not to become too thin in places nor too compressed. Ten days hammering is needed to make a vase. For twenty hours each stroke must be exactly like the others. The steadier and more even the hammering, the more perfect and beautiful will be the form. Yet despite the slowness of the process the pupil must continuously watch the form his object is taking and adjust his work accordingly. In doing so he learns to develop stamina.

Woodwork is different again. The pupils have already discovered in Grades 5 and 6 that in many cases it is only necessary to bring out the grain and branching of a piece of wood to create a little work of art. A wooden animal made by rasping such a piece can be highly original if the light and dark shades of the wood are skilfully used. In carving a piece of gnarled poplar, those who understand this mysterious "language" can feel how the grain suggests a human form; they only have to accentuate it by making a few cuts. Carving also teaches them how different are the various kinds of wood. The knife must be applied differently when carving soft poplar or hard oak. Equally different is the way in which the shavings come off. In planing, too, the differences in grain can be felt under the plane. Each kind of wood reveals to the carver its fast or slow growth, its moisture or dryness calling for varying degrees of accuracy and finish.

To sum up, working at the forge trains powers of decision, copperwork develops a feeling for form and space as well as rhythmic mobility, while woodwork involves perception of the finer characteristics of the material. If the pupils were allowed to choose among these activities, they would simply follow their own inclinations. But since a harmonious promotion of all their potentialities can only occur if they also practise doing what they do not particularly like, all these courses are compulsory for every pupil.

2.4.6 *Curricular goals of the practical activities*

These goals are:

- to cultivate the interest in discovering and experimenting, which is characteristic of this age group, by combining specialized instruction and exact work with the processes of understanding and learning;

- to familiarize the adolescent with the production and functions of implements in everyday use,

such as electric irons, standard lamps, electrical installations, soap, small furniture items, nets, etc.;
- to verbalize these practical activities through written and oral descriptions, thus connecting the verbal culture of the School with areas of practical experience typical of the households in the environment;
- to train the pupils in frequently required manual skills and correct use of instruments, such as the handling of glass tubes and scales in the chemical laboratory, and of drills and measuring instruments in the smithy;
- to extend the pupils' perceptive power, until then practised mainly in the artistic domain, to objectively verifiable observation of fine technical details, such as precise angles and accurate fit. This will also be of help in future science work;
- to develop a thorough understanding of the characteristics of common objects and a consciousness of competence in certain fields, as a foundation for self-confidence based on experience and insight which will enable the pupils to tackle unknown matters with calmness and assurance.

Not all these objectives can be pursued in one block period. The various practical periods must complement each other (see Fig.7).

The teachers' reports which follow will illustrate how the academic, artistic and practical lessons in Grades 9 and 10 are designed to meet the special needs of this age group.

## 2.4.7 Blacksmith's work

First the class must learn the fundamentals of the craft, i.e. handling the hearth and the tools and controlling the fire. That is not easy as it requires an understanding of the technical equipment. In this preparatory phase some items previously dealt with in vocational study lessons, such as ore extraction, crude iron production, modern methods of steel production, are briefly recapitulated. The instructor brings them

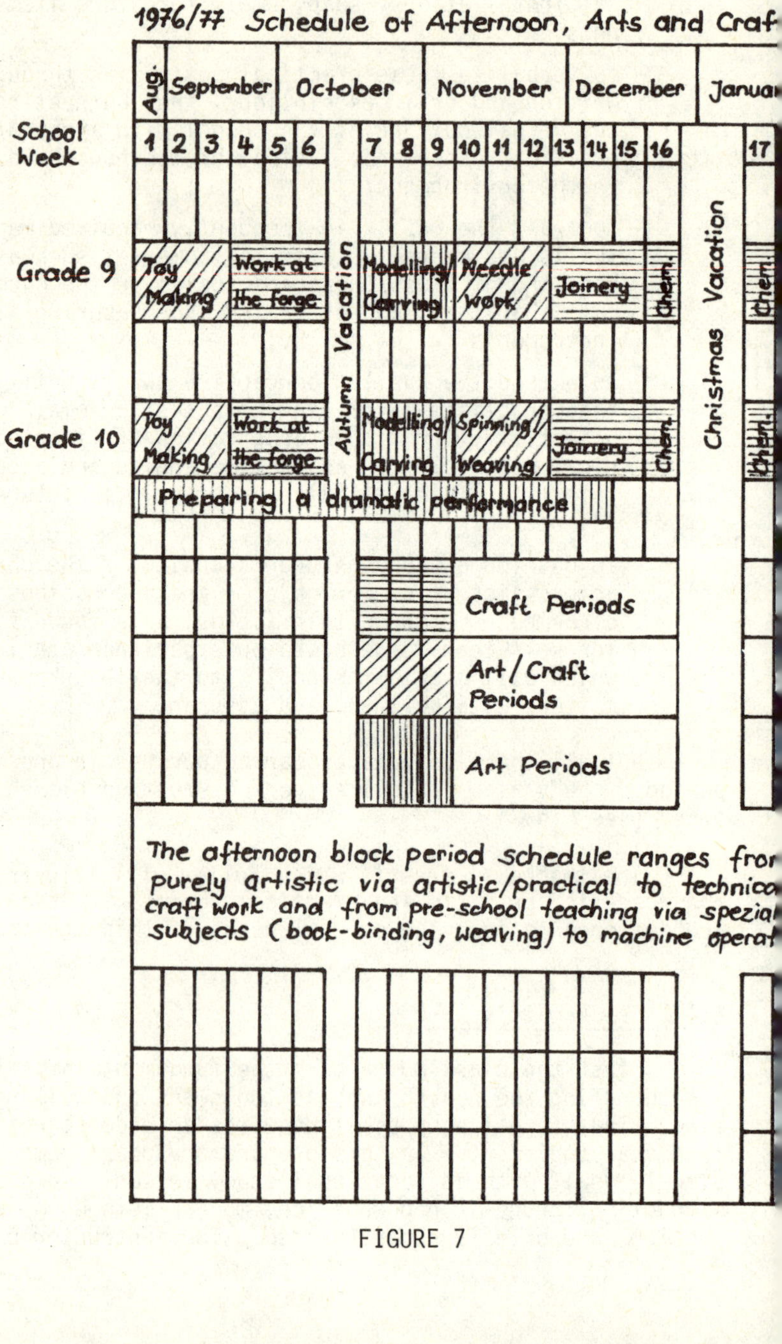

1976/77 Schedule of Afternoon, Arts and Craft

|  | Aug. | September | October | November | December | January |
|---|---|---|---|---|---|---|
| School Week | 1 | 2 3 4 5 6 | 7 8 9 10 11 12 13 | 14 15 16 | | 17 |

Grade 9: Toy Making / Work at the forge / Autumn Vacation / Modelling Carving / Needle work / Joinery / Chem. / Christmas Vacation / Chem.

Grade 10: Toy Making / Work at the forge / Modelling Carving / Spinning Weaving / Joinery / Chem. / Chem.

Preparing a dramatic performance

- Craft Periods
- Art/Craft Periods
- Art Periods

The afternoon block period schedule ranges from purely artistic via artistic/practical to technical craft work and from pre-school teaching via special subjects (book-binding, weaving) to machine operat

FIGURE 7

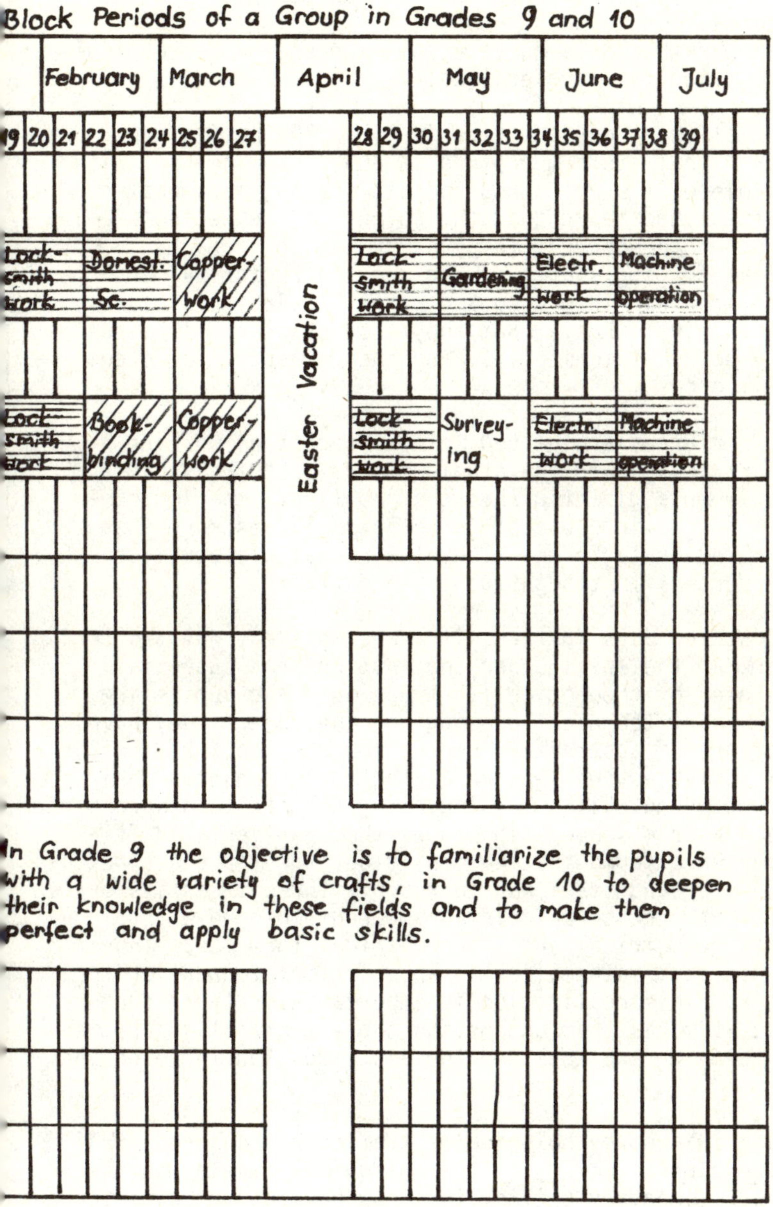

Block Periods of a Group in Grades 9 and 10

| February | March | April | May | June | July |
|---|---|---|---|---|---|
| 19 20 21 22 23 24 25 26 27 | | 28 29 30 31 32 33 34 35 36 37 38 39 | | | |

Lock-smith work | Domest. Sc. | Copper-work | Easter Vacation | Lock-smith work | Gardening | Electr. work | Machine operation

Lock-smith work | Book-binding | Copper-work | | Lock-smith work | Survey-ing | Electr. work | Machine operation

In Grade 9 the objective is to familiarize the pupils with a wide variety of crafts, in Grade 10 to deepen their knowledge in these fields and to make them perfect and apply basic skills.

FIGURE 7

to life by giving demonstrations at the hearth and recounting examples from his personal experience. Thus the pupils begin to see the connection between theoretical vocational studies and practical workshop procedures. Some concepts and technical terms are only then fully understood.

On the following day the fire is lit. The pupils are amazed to learn that its temperature is $3000^o$ C. They see with wonder how a piece of steel turns redhot, scales, incinerates or even gasifies, and learn that the colour of the heated steel indicates whether the correct temperature has been reached. Then the actual forging starts. When the instructor hammers the end of an iron bar into a square point, their faces clearly show what they think: Easy! But they soon change their minds when they try doing it themselves, and their respect for steel worker's skill grows.

Many experiences are gained in the process of working. Some pupils are too slow; the steel gets cold. Others hammer too timidly. When a girl finishes the job first, the "muscle-men" see that disciplined use of force accomplishes more than does uncontrolled brute force. They learn that a blacksmith must combine force with thoughtfulness and stamina.

The first few days in the smithy are entirely devoted to practical work at the anvil under the instructor's supervision. They are followed by theoretical instruction. The pupils are asked to make exact technical drawings of the object they have made. The effort of abstraction needed for this task reinforces their mental abilities, while work at the forge enhances their physical strength and skills. Calculating the bar length required to make a cone-shaped tip causes them particular difficulties. They have found that hammering out the top end stretches that piece of round steel bar to roughly three times its original length, but precise calculations cannot be done without using abstract geometrical and stereometrical formulas. Thus they experience that mathematics is an essential foundation for practical work. This realization is important for their further education, as it makes them understand the interrelations between the various teaching subjects and the justification for each one of them.

In Grade 10 the psychological situation has changed. While in Grade 9 the pupils' energy and attention was riveted to the acquisition of elementary skills, they now have enough experience and detachment from the actual manipulation to plan their own

work and produce more ambitious items, such as chisels, candle-
holders, triangles, fire tongs, or key brackets. In the three-
stage process of planning, execution and checking they learn
the basic requirements of technical rationality in this field.
They also learn teamwork. For the production of large or difficult objects the work is divided between two, one hammering
and the other guiding the workpiece on the anvil. This gives
them immediate experience of how each one depends on the partner's knowledge, skill and reliability. Moreover, in each phase
the connection of the team's work with the whole is evident.
Thus insights and abilities indispensable in our civilization
with its division of labour are developed.

At the forge human qualities are practised - not in general talk but in a very concrete manner. The workpiece itself
speaks only too clearly; the instructor merely has to draw
attention to what has been well or badly done. In their con-
frontation with the impersonal material the young people exercise attitudes and behaviours which will later help them to
forge their own destiny.
                                            Berthold May


2.4.8 *Locksmith's work in Grade 9*

The truth of the German adage "Iron educates" becomes
still more evident in locksmith's work. After the first five
minutes of filing the pupils know that steel is harder than
butter. It takes a long time to file off 1 mm of steel or to
saw through a piece. Since at the same time attention must be
paid to measurements, angles and evenness of surface, the tools
must be guided with great care. Some pupils have to make a considerable effort to visualize the finished product from the
technical drawing on the board. In the lower grades they had
seen the form it should have; now in their imagination they
have to convert a two-dimensional drawing into a three-dimensional object with corners, bore holes, notches, etc. at different levels. This is a complicated process. To execute the
job they need a steel rule and a calliper.

By the end of the second block period they must be able
to work to specifications down to one twentieth of a millimeter.
Some of them wonder whether such precision is necessary. They
get their answer when two of them have to make a dual pipe clamp,
each producing one part of it, or when in the second block
period spare parts for an excavator have to be made and fitted.

While in the first block period the emphasis is on acquiring elementary skill in filing and measuring, in the second period the focus is on division of labour. For instance, a team of three pupils has to produce a simple sliding bolt. One makes the base plate, the second the two keeps and the third the bolt. It seems easy enough, but in trying to fit the parts together it is often found that either the bolt does not go through, so that more precise filing of the bolt or the keeps is necessary, or that it virtually falls through, in which case the whole construction has to be scrapped - a wholesome lesson.

In this work the pupils gain three basic insights. They see that, where a task can be sensibly divided, such division of labour offers considerable advantages; more and higher-quality articles will be produced than would be the case if each individual made entire ones. They also see that division of labour is impossible without strict adherence by everyone concerned to agreed measurements and norms. And they accept technical drawings as a suitable means of laying down specifications of shapes, measurements and qualitites. It becomes clear to them that the entire job will be useless if just one individual does not work with complete accuracy.

Hans Becker and Heinz Schmidt

2.4.9 *Grade 9 make wooden boxes*

In Grades 5-8 the pupils learnt how to handle wood and tools. Now they are asked to build a wooden box with insets. Whether it should be a sewing box or one for shoe polish and brushes, and what its measurements should be, is left to them to decide. The only condition is that one or more smaller boxes should be fitted into it. This means that each pupil must think for himself; he can no longer merely copy his neighbour's piece or the instructor's demonstration. He must reflect: where will the box be kept at home? That determines its measurements. What is going to be put into it? That determines its interior construction. The constraints imposed, not by the instructor but by the object itself, become very obvious when a mistake has been made, such as inaccurate measurement, faulty sawing, excessive planing. There is no need for the instructor to point out such mistakes; the object gives indisputable evidence.

2.4.10 _Electrical work in Grade 9_

In the second half of the electricity block period a pupil brings along a vacuum cleaner which had interfered with the television reception at his home and then failed to operate altogether. The pupils try to guess what might be the cause of the trouble. Then the instructor shows them the correct way of examining a defective electrical instrument to locate a fault. Together they find that the carbons are worn out and that the collector is dirty. This means putting in new carbons and cleaning the collector. The examination also reveals worn insulation and near-defective solderings which should be repaired.

The pupils then return to the switchgear on their practice boards, except for the boy with the vacuum cleaner who is allowed to repair it because he has already finished his installation job. The others are still learning how to insulate a wire end, bend it into a loop and fix it to the switch. The wires must not criss-cross; they must all lie vertically or horizontally on the board. Switch and socket must be placed directly below the distribution box, at the standard distance from the floor and the door frame. The pupils must not only understand various types of switch (on-off switch, change-over switch, serial switch, intermediate switch), but must also remember which colour of insulating tape is used for each kind of wire.

One girl who was at first reluctant to take part because she felt she would never understand all this, soon found that she was cleverer than many of the boys in handling the wires. She also discovered that a cracked electric socket at her home was a change-over switch, and she bought and installed a new one. A boy who was particularly good at applying what he had learnt, installed the complete electrical circuit in his new house together with his father. He was able to show him how to do a number of things and to explain to him the various kinds of change-over switch that are available.

After two weeks of this block period all the pupils were engaged in repairing table lamps, standard lamps, electric irons, vacuum cleaners, hotplates or electric fires they had brought from home. When it was found that the hotplate had to be rewired, they all got together to discuss the problem of how to determine the resistance of the wire from its diameter, length and composition. Working out a suitable mathematical formula, and then converting it to obtain the required length of wire, proved much more difficult than calculating with x and y in mathematics lessons.  Even good "mathematicians" found it far from easy to apply their theoretical knowledge to this practical workshop problem.

Heinz Schmidt

## 2.4.11 Chemistry block period in Grade 9

When a group of pupils enter the laboratory, the teacher notes that some, especially the girls, seem rather intimidated at the sight of so many bottles of chemicals, the fire extinguishers and the protective glasses, while most of the boys feel perfectly at home in the lab.

First, pieces of tubing glass are heated redhot and then bent or drawn into simple laboratory implements.  Gradually the pupils develop a feel for the right degree of heat and softness of the glass.  At the price of many a blister they shed their timidity and clumsiness and learn how to handle glass, the material with which they will have to work in the next few weeks.

One objective of these chemistry periods is to train powers of observation.  To give an example:  tin is to be produced out of cassiterite.  The pupils have to mix defined quantities of active coal powder, cassiterite, sodium carbonate and potash.  In heating the matt, dark grey mixture in a crucible, they can observe how it first turns a slightly lighter colour, and a gas ejecting some of the substance escapes at a few points. Soon a "pulsating" process starts:  The condensing and transforming mass is breathing rhythmically.  When it expels gas it contracts throwing off sparks.  Little craters in the melting mass at the bottom of the crucible glow in a dark red, which eventually spreads over the whole content.  For the first time the pupils see the final product, the glowing red metal in the midst of the melting flow.  This is then poured onto a metal plate to cool and set into a silvery, shining metal - tin.

The pupils must first learn to absorb the whole range and sequence of observations that can be made during such an experiment without considering the final outcome.  If they fixed their attention on that, they would regard the processes and observations as either important or unimportant from the point of view of the end result.

On the following day, when the pupils have slept on the experience, they try to find explanations.  But as they endeavour to remember everything it becomes clear that they recall different things, and that even their observations of the same detail differ. They realize how much they have failed to observe, and are surprised to see how many new details they notice when the experiment is repeated. In comparing their observations with those of other pupils they learn to depersonalize their perceptions and at the same time to differentiate and enrich their stock of concepts.

Another help in training the power of observation is to make drawings of interesting experiments. For instance, to illustrate the process involved in the formation of a solution, a pupil is told to let a drop of a coloured substance fall into a liquid from just above the surface. On touching the surface the drop changes its shape. Usually it forms an inward-turning ring which expands as it sinks down. Gradually the ring thickens in places into blobs connected by arches, which sink more swiftly, forming new rings in the process which in turn divide into blobs. Thus the drop continues permeating the liquid until a solution is obtained. The pupils' task now is to observe and draw the various phases of the process in chronological order. Gaps in their observation or memory must be filled by appropriate imagination. This exercise does not encourage arbitrariness but strengthens the powers of recall and observation.

Hermann Aleff

2.4.12 *Drawing and painting lessons in Grades 9 and 10*

In Grade 9 drawing and painting lessons are no longer given by the class teacher but by a specialist. This implies a new teaching method corresponding to the 15-16 year olds' need for independence. In the lower grades they had been given thorough practice in painting with water colours. On the basis of Goethe's "Colour Theory" they learnt the laws of colour by mixing on their papers the basic colours yellow, blue and red into whatever shade they wanted for painting motifs from animal or nature study or geography. Now they are inclined to throw overboard everything they have learnt under the teacher's guidance.

Most of them are fascinated by the technical production of pictures, which seems to them more rational than artistic composition. On the other hand, they are also eager to engage in free artistic activity, to use their own imagination. For the teacher this poses a problem. Knowing that systematic practice is indispensable for artistic work, he must find a way of guiding them into a creative process where they can carry out selected tasks in their individual manner. At that age adolescents live in constant inner conflict. It is therefore appropriate for them to occupy themselves with chiaroscuro, the world of light and darkness, which also ties in with their interest in the rational and unequivocal. In Grades 6 and 7 they have learnt shadowing, making charcoal drawings of simple objects; they have studied the relationships of light source, object and shade. All this now serves as a basis for artistic rendering of more complicated subjects in charcoal, graphite or ink.

Observation and careful differentiation of grades of darkness are required to understand the light and shade relationships of three-dimensional objects standing on a surface and illuminated from one side. The pupils enjoy puzzling out how a circle can gradually be turned into a spherical body through shading. There is a host of degrees of lightness as well as of contrasts between light and dark. In exploring them their hands get practice in drawing regular grey areas shading off into lighter or darker ones, and at the same time the original, rational estimation of shades develops into a live feeling for the mysterious chiaroscuro. This is of great importance for the growth of imaginative powers.

At puberty the children's originally bubbling imagination gradually subsides. It must be revitalized in order to infuse feeling into their awakening forces of abstraction and precision. A task requiring careful observation, clarification of relationships and their conversion into light and shade provides an ideal stimulus.

The fully artistic domain is entered when a masterpiece, such as Dürer's engraving "Melancholia", is reproduced as a charcoal drawing. Dürer's realistic presentation with its wealth of interesting, partly enigmatic, symbolic detail immediately appeals to most pupils. At first some details are drawn and the composition is studied with the help of the teacher. Soon the pupils discover that the discussion of such a work of art opens their eyes to the impression conveyed by certain form elements, and this realization leads them far beyond their own powers of expression. Finally, after many lessons, they create an enlarged version of the "Melancholia" in which the composition as a whole is reproduced, while some details are left out.

To avoid getting into a routine, the pupils, who have by then acquired a good deal of drawing technique, are asked to reproduce a Rembrandt etching in ink. In this work they experience a far more dynamic, unfettered use of chiaroscuro. The deep black of the ink offers an adequate means of expression. The execution is again directed by their inner experience of the picture and by their understanding of its necessities. Although the teacher still contributes to this understanding, the pupils are guided by their own conception rather than by his judgement. Their feelings of like or dislike quickly give way to an exploration of the Why of an artistic solution. It is, therefore, important to choose timeless masterpieces for these activities.

Exercises of this kind also promote an understanding of the history of art and the sciences. The pupils actually experience, and to a certain extent comprehend, the vast changes art has undergone in its development from Dürer to Rembrandt.

After this intensive occupation with chiaroscuro the pupils naturally feel a desire for colour. The painting lessons also start with systematic practice. Goethe's colour circle is painted in the wet-in-wet technique, in which the colours merge into each other. Then comes layer practice: the first layer of watercolour must be quite dry before the second layer is put on. Though some pupils are unable to master the self-discipline this technique demands, all do experience the greater brilliance and variety of colours as well as the need for more condensed composition. With this experience Grade 10 can then attempt to convert an engraving by Dürer or Rembrandt into colour. This recognizing the colour equivalents of greys and translating the mood of the picture into colour.

In these two years of systematic practice the pupils become independent in their judgement. They enrich and train their sensory perception and their feeling and acquire a command of various techniques which will enable them to progress in Grades 11 and 12 to individual, free artistic expression.

Ekkehard Heyder

## 2.4.13 *Locksmith's work in Grade 10*

The instructor sketches on the blackboard a technical drawing of a spacer, 1 mm in thickness, with two drill holes. An industrial company has ordered 50 of these from the school workshop. In the discussion on how best to manufacture them one pupil suggests stacking the 50 sheets and drilling them together. Another proposes inventing a tool which will hold them firmly in position to ensure that each spacer will precisely meet the specification. A calculation of the time required to construct such a tool as compared to that needed to trace, grain and debur 50 separate sheets and drill 100 separate holes at precisely the same distance confirm the advantages of the proposed method, quite apart from the fact that it is much more interesting to design and build something new than to spend hours on monotonous manual work. A problem arises in calculating how the tolerances will add up in the pile of sheets, since the total must not exceed a definite figure. With the aid of tolerance and fitting tables the whole construction is reconsidered, and then the work is distributed. Each pupil will manufacture one part, of which he will first make a drawing and then a work plan indicating the sequence of operations and the tools required. It is noticeable that in this block period the pupils have a better command of working techniques, greater precision and more independence in planning and execution than they had at the end of the previous period. Even the girls, who were at first less interested, show manual ability and, in general, work more conscientiously and correctly than the boys.

When the finished parts are assembled, each pupil watches eagerly to see whether his own will fit. There is one flaw. Two vertical screws are too wide apart at the top. An investigation reveals that the distance is correct at the bottom, but the screws have not been welded quite vertically into the ground plate. The fault is corrected, and then the whole manufacturing process is reviewed. The time actually spent on the work by each pupil is compared with the estimate. Some are astonished to find that they have needed three times the estimated amount. They try to discover why, and their respect for skilled workers producing the schedule grows.

Meanwhile another group has prepared the 50 spacers except for the drilling. Almost ceremoniously they are placed into the new instrument. To everybody's delight it functions perfectly. The drilling is done in a short time, all the holes are clean and correctly spaced.

Thus the pupils have taken the step from crafts production to industrial production. In constructing a simple machine tool they have discovered the usefulness of division of labour. They have also learnt that rational technical manufacture requires a division into planning, execution and control stages.

In accordance with their age they have experienced, in a complete process, the mode of production they will later encounter in the highly specialized work organization of industry.

Werner Rafhöfer

## 2.4.14 Machine operation in Grades 9 and 10

In the first machine operation period at the end of Grade 9 the instructor explains the lathe and demonstrates its operation by turning a piston for a hydraulic press. He informs the pupils that DM 2000 worth of damage is done if the support is not switched off at the right moment and the steel cuts into the lathe chuck. He also shows them how to use dial gauges and micrometer slide rules and discusses fit and fitting systems, a very complicated subject.

Then ancillary jobs are distributed. One pupil has to see that the oil cans are always full, another has to clear away the shavings, a girl is put in charge of the record sheet, etc. There is a job for everybody.

On the third day the pupils start operating the machines. One over-confident boy gets so carried away by his delight in operating his lathe that he forgets all about the stipulated tolerances for the cylindrical pieces he is making, and cuts off too much. In the second week, he has a "bright idea". Eager to work faster than prescribed, he sets the controls to a higher rotation speed and feeding rate, with the result that the surface of his workpiece is ruined and the cutting tool, which had run too hot, is also damaged. The class is then called together to discuss the interrelation between rotation speed, feed rate, surface condition and temperature of the lathe tool. They also realize how and why the shavings come off in a certain shape, forming a nice spiral or breaking off. Finally, the correct way of utilizing a "bright idea" is discussed.

In the third week, the same pupil worked on a shaping machine making spare parts for a cement mixer, and at the end of the second block period in Grade 10 he was able to produce 30 rollers for an escalator ordered by an outside firm to specifications requiring a precision of 1/200 mm.

In these block periods the pupils learn to operate a variety of machines and get to know their exact nature and functioning. Although they produce parts only, the preceding lessons in which they manufactured complete products have kept alive their interest in the purpose of these parts.

Günter Reichert

## 2.4.15 Vocational studies in Grade 10. Industrial processes

As an example of industrial production, the manufacture of a car is studied in this block period. The class goes to the car park to look at various makes. One car is driven out and thoroughly examined, inside and out: the power transmission from motor to drive wheels, the cooling system, steering, battery and chassis. Then the development of automobiles from the beginning of motoring is discussed. Hearing of the tenacity and willpower of the pioneers who persevered in their efforts undeterred by setbacks makes a great impression on the pupils and makes the age of horsedrawn carriages come alive to them.

In a discussion of technical achievements not only the advantages, but also the hazards involved must be mentioned. Diametrically opposed statements on the subject, such as Georg Jünger's "Even the smallest technical work process uses up more power than it produces" and Friedrich Dessauer's "Is technical work really the devil's invention if it provides millions of people with the means of existence?" are considered in the light of Dessauer's calculation that in 1926, 2 million to 2.5 million slaves would have been necessary to maintain our way of life without energy-producing machinery. If our technical manufacture, our trains, lighting and water systems were to continue as at present without the use of motors, 2,000 million people would have to spend their entire lives turning drive wheels, lifting and carrying loads. In the past, many people did actually have to do such work all their lives. From their own experience in the workshops the pupils know the effort required to saw, file, chisel or forge by hand, and they also know how easy all this becomes when a machine does the hard work.

In an experiment with a screw press the pupils see how steel sheeting is almost effortlessly transformed, illustrating the "Golden Rule of Mechanics" they had learnt in physics lessons: "Small (manual) force applied over a long distance (rotation) equals great force (press) over a short distance". The pupils recognize this principle when working at the various machine tools in the workshop. On the basis of the data measured on these machines they solve problems about cutting speed, feed rate, belt drive, gear drive, planing, drilling, milling, etc. Having learnt from their own experiences in the workshops that any mistake in calculation will have serious consequences, they now realize how important mathematical practice is.

Knowledge of geometry must be applied in making drawings of cutting or penetration curves of cylindrical or cone-shaped machine parts. Thinking in three-dimensional terms must be developed.

The pupils' recent experience of division of labour for the construction of a clamping instrument for spacers has prepared them for a visit to an automobile factory, where the splitting up of the work process into a large number of specialized jobs achieves maximum output and labour yield with minimum expenditure of time and energy. As the boys and girls have already acquired essential basic knowledge of the construction and functioning of combustion engines at school, they are able to follow the production process at the factory. The sheer size and variety of the machinery, as well as the smooth work organization, impress them deeply.

Visits of this kind show that the pupils' own practical experience facilitates their comprehension of corresponding large-scale processes and gives them an immediate understanding of the rationality of a system dividing the work into highly specialized operations. Moreover, they see how the workers must function as parts of a production system that is planned down to the last detail. This human aspect is later dealt with in the social study lessons.

Herbert Mosner

2.4.16 *Mathematics and surveying in Grade 10*

On a warm, sunny autumn afternoon, two hours before low tide, the class set out for a 5 km walk across the mud flats to the bird holm Norderoog. Crossing the tidal gully near the shore they had to wade kneedeep through water. Then they walked for an hour across mud, shell reefs and stretches of sand interspersed with pools of water. On the holm the bird warden showed them the traces of the birds breeding there in the summer, including some rare species of sea-martins and oyster-catchers. On the way back, with the sun behind them, they admired the clear horizon and the magnificent colouring of the clouds and the holm against the setting sun.

Surveying activities are embedded in experiences of nature

such as this. One pear-shaped holm, with an area of 591 hectares and a circumference of 13 km, is inhabited by 190 people whose houses stand on 10 mounds regularly spaced out on the islet. Using these mounds as corner points, the entire holm was covered on a chart with a network of triangles. The 43 pupils in the class were divided into groups of four or five, and each group had to carry out a variety of surveying tasks. Stone dykes, roads and tidal gullies had to be entered on the sides of the triangle net-work. Measurements of angles and distances, to a precision of one half of an angular minute and 1 cm respectively, formed the basis for trigonometrical calculations, which then served to check the measuring results. No unchecked result was allowed to be used for the maps (scale 1:2000 or 1:4000) which every pupil had to make of the section surveyed by his group. From these sectional maps each pupil had to produce an overall map of the islet (scale 1:7000).

Appropriate trigonometrical calculation and construction methods were worked out in the main lessons in the morning and subsequently tried out in new tasks. First, the fundamental lines and triangles were measured by everyone. If the results diverged, which they often did, the measuring was repeated. The indifference towards mistakes displayed by many pupils in mathematics lessons had entirely disappeared. Once they had found out how many kinds of mistake can be made and how much additional work they cause, the groups could begin their separate tasks.

The most difficult part was precision measuring with the theodolite. But when they had learnt how to manipulate the various adjusting devices - to the surprise of the boys, some of the girls learnt this very quickly and accurately - it was fun working with such a precision instrument. At the same time, they practised estimating distances and angles. The pupils were keen to see just how correctly they could guess. After a week's practice, any estimate that was far off the mark was greeted with general laughter.

The groups had to be well balanced, not only in terms of boys and girls, but also of talents. Each should, if possible, include one practical person, one good mathematician, one stickler for accuracy. Forgetfulness soon cured itself; forgetting to bring a tool along meant walking a distance of 2 km each way to fetch it, and incurring the anger of the group.

New criteria also entered into the pupils' evaluation of

each other: Who furthered the group through consistent, solid work? Who did nothing useful, thus burdening the other group members with extra work? As a result, the social structure of the class shifted. Pupils who liked to catch crabs or otherwise enjoy themselves instead of working were detailed by their comrades to carry poles, run to and fro to align implements, and do similar unpopular jobs.

Each group in rotation had to do the house work and prepare the meals under the supervision of two domestic science teachers. Thus they learnt how to cook for a large group, and how to cope swiftly and efficiently with the usual domestic chores. In the evenings all set together to listen to tales of the islet and its inhabitants, of floods and storms, of areas now submerged or torn off by raging seas and of the people's sufferings on such occasions. Once a class actually experienced a flooding which cut them off from the mainland on the day scheduled for their departure, and as their provisions had been used up they felt what it is like to be marooned.

The overall objectives of the surveying period are the following:

1) to make the pupils see the need for calculation and verification of results. The mathematical areas involved are logarithmic calculations with sine and cosine theorem and related procedures;

2) to provide for boys and girls who find it difficult to understand complicated theory an access to mathematics via its practical aspect which demonstrates the need for accuracy and reliability;

3) to offer the 16 year olds, who are interested not only in understanding interconnections but also in applying them, a challenge demanding full use of their intelligence, and thus to help them attain an independence founded on proven competence;

4) to familiarize the adolescents with maps and their production;

5) to assist them in gaining new human and social standards. The group work gives them an opportunity to develop sound judgements of themselves and of others in a neutral, objective way.

Peter Bütow

## 2.4.17 *Toy making in Grade 10. Dolls*

In a three week course lasting 2 hours 15 minutes every day, boys and girls make dolls of various sizes. While the objective of the toy-making block period in Grade 6 (see 2.3.8) had been to familiarize the pupils with the proportions and functioning of human and animal bodies, the emphasis in this course for 16 year olds is on producing toys that are suitable for the children who will play with them. The social aspect thus predominates. The pupils' work is no longer determined by their own requirements but by the actual needs of children in the kindergarten.

They try to remember what kinds of doll they had liked best when they were that age. Even the boys admit, after some hesitation, that they liked playing with teddy bears and even with dolls. In this discussion they come to realize that the perfect, fashionable dolls usually offered leave the child too little room for exercising his imagination. The dolls they were going to make would be soft and pliable and offer many opportunities for variation, so that the children could themselves endow them with a life of their own, make them laugh or cry according to their own mood.

The pupils start with the simplest form, a tissue paper doll with a head, trunk and limbs. It should be able to stand. The pupils find how difficult it is to handle the thin paper and to create harmonious proportions, to make the figurines lifelike and movable. In comparing their own creations with those of their classmates they gain more detachment from their own work and learn to judge that of the others more objectively.

On the next day soft fabric dolls for infants are made. One side of a piece of plain material is bunched into a head, the two neighbouring corners form the arms and the other two the legs. All the needlework techniques the pupils have learnt (sewing by hand or machine, embroidering, knitting) can be used in the process, providing further practice in these skills.

The following task, making small movable dolls for pre-school children, practises team work. Wire is shaped into skeletons with movable limbs and covered with raw wool. The clothing is made of bright material. Again the pupils learn that each material demands a special kind of treatment. The hard copper wire must be bent with pliers; wool, soft and warm, is easy to work with and pleasant for the child to touch; linen is stiffer, more suitable for larger dolls; silk is difficult to sew but attractive and smooth for the child's hands. As the size of the doll must match the dolls' houses the 9th grade has made, exact measuring and fitting is necessary.

Moreover, each individual's work must fit into the whole. Many pupils in Grade 10 find this difficult, since their behaviour is still entirely self-centred. It is a healthy learning process for them to experience the necessity of subordinating themselves to the demands of a joint effort, regardless of personal sympathy or antipathy.

Christine Britsche

## 2.4.18 *Poetry block period in Grade 10*

In the first of the upper grades a new subject, art appreciation, is introduced. Following on from the practical art and craft activities in which the pupils have engaged throughout the preceding school years, they are now to be acquainted with masterpieces that will serve as standards and teach them the concept and metamorphosis of beauty as well as the historical evolution of artistic expression. In Grade 9 they study the development of the arts from the old Egyptian to the Rembrandt period; in Grade 10 the emphasis is on language and poetry. Always the entire domain of artistic creation is kept in view. This systematically developed understanding of art is intended to counterbalance the abstraction and rationality involved in comprehending the laws of nature, which is the foremost concern of that age-group.

In the poetry period the forms and rules of poetry are studied. What is needed at this stage is depth of understanding rather than breadth of knowledge. The pupils' existing personal relationship to poetry is to be intensified, for art, more than any other domain, is apt to make them aware of their individual inclinations. Such awareness enhances self-confidence and thus helps them to develop a more profound feeling of identity.

Ever since the first grade the pupils have experienced a wide range of poetry in their choral and recitation practice, in eurhythmy and dramatics. To transform this sensory and emotional experience into cognitive appreciation and deep understanding, works of art are now analyzed and reflected upon. Language is studied as a material. The pupils learn to differentiate between colloquial language and literary language and to distinguish the instruments of poetry, such as rhythm, metre, sound, rhyme, metaphor and poetic genre. The study material is chosen by the pupils themselves. They bring along poems they particularly like or desire to understand better.

When the whole field of poetry has thus been explored to some extent, the application of these poetic instruments is studied in individual poems. From the successive versions of C.F. Meyer's "Der römische Brunnen" (The Roman Fountain) the pupils learn to discern qualitative differences and to develop critical appreciation. Whereas the several versions of this poem show how the thought content finds ever more poignant expression through condensation of form until a crystal clear version is achieved, Brentano's "Abendständchen" (Serenade) provides a typical example of the essence of lyricism.

Since to us Europeans Homer's epics constitute the archetype of epic poetry, an episode from the 19th book of the *Odyssey* is chosen for study. The teacher recites the passage where Ulysses returns to Ithaca. His old nurse does not recognize him, treats him as a guest and washes his feet, as was the custom. In doing so she recognizes him by a scar on his foot. At this point the sequence of events is interrupted by several hundred lines describing in great detail how the young Ulysses got this scar when hunting boars on his grandfather's land, with some genealogical information thrown in. When the narrative returns to the old woman who is so excited by her discovery that she lets Ulysses's foot drop back into the water, very few pupils remember that the story had broken off with her lifting the foot up to wash it. Now the question arises why Homer made this lengthy insertion. As a retarding element to heighten tension it is far too long. In the discussion the pupils realize that Homer had no particular purpose in mind, that he merely recounted, leisurely and colourfully, what he knew of his people's history. Comparing their impression with that evoked by lyrical poems, they arrive at the formulation: in a lyrical poem the poet expresses his thoughts and feelings directly; in an epic he recounts memories from a spatial and temporal distance, and this applies even to modern prose describing events in the present.

The study of drama centers on Kleist's "Der zerbrochene Krug" (The Broken Jug). An analysis of form, as attempted in the lyrical poetry period, cannot be undertaken within the limits of a block period on epic or drama. Moreover, the pupils are more interested in the basic human attitudes determining a poet's choice of a particular genre. Kleist demonstrates vividly that drama expresses an active will in conflict with an adversary, while Homer, an epic poet, observes the world from the outside, knitting events together into a fabric of thoughts, and lyrical poets express themselves as individuals. Starting from these three distinctions the pupils, who at that age like clear formulations which help them to differentiate, tried to establish further relationships. They found that lyrics relate to the present, epics to the past, and drama to the future, not only because the action remains open-ended, but because the will inspiring it is directed towards the new, the outcome it will entail.

There is also a grammatical distinction. Lyrics are dominated by the I, drama by the Thou, and epics by the third person. Such sharp formulation reveals, however, that these distinctions do not apply absolutely. Though they predominate in the respective basic genres, all three forms exist to a greater or lesser extent in each.

Not until relationships of this kind have been worked out do the pupils see the exemplary nature of a work such as Kleist's drama. The plot's concentration on injustice would make it appear almost inhumanly ruthless, if a slightly humorous treatment did not indicate that the villain's behaviour stems from human weakness. Considerations of this nature remind the pupils of experiences they themselves have had. There is then no need for the teacher to point out that an unruffled, observing attitude and empathy can considerably improve a tense situation. Though it may be difficult to put this insight into practice at the right moment, awareness of the possibility already has a liberating effect.

Hans Martin Büche

2.4.19 *Dramatics in Grade 10*

a) Curricular value of dramatics

Dramatics is a regular part of the Waldorf curriculum. It is seen as an opportunity to discover the self in an artistic process through playing, and thus experiencing, new roles. Practice in acting develops hidden forces of imagination and will.

In Grade 10 the objectives of dramatic performances differ from those pursued in earlier years. 16 and 17 year olds frequently find themselves in the throes of inner conflict. On the one hand, they are buffeted by recently discovered emotional forces and drives, on the other hand they feel a strong need and an emerging capacity to understand the laws governing the diversity of the world in its manifold manifestations, to see interconnections and interactions. Consequently their moods and behaviour oscillate between keenness and lassitude. Sometimes they seem to explode with internal or external involvement, at other times they are emotionally blocked up or deeply depressed. While dominated by changing moods, they may be astonishingly sober in their mathematics, science or craft work. Often they are sharply critical, rash in their judgement, sometimes smug in their attitude to human weaknesses and inadequacies.

Acting offers an opportunity to do justice to both the emotional urges of the adolescents and their need for understanding. It absorbs their active critical ability and transforms it into constructive criticism. The stage itself becomes the place where all these feelings will be displayed. The emotional inner world is enticed to come out into the open so that it may find release, correction and purification in the interplay of forces, inclinations, challenges and obligations. In dramatics these drives do not run rampant, they become visible and transparent as a field of opposing tensions. This new level of reality, fully penetrated as it is by consciousness, demands the involvement of the whole person. Each pupil must work seriously to improve

- his powers of imagination, in order to develop a dramatic character with its typical ways of behaviour and action into a life-like, rounded individual and to construct a precise idea of the course of the dramatic action;

- his motor activity, in order to enable his entire body - head, trunk, limbs - to become an instrument of expression which will react spontaneously and at the same time be controlled;

- his speech, which has to render the resonance, impact and expressive force of individual sounds and the cadence of the syllables while following the special rhythmic laws of prose and verse.

b) Understanding of dramatic rules

The pupils must be guided to the recognition that drama has its objective rules, that every small detail matters. The dialogue reveals the polar tension and the dialectic dynamics of play and counterplay, the duelling situation. It is governed by the dramatic rule of interaction. A king is only sovereign to the extent that his subjects' subservience allows him to be. Dramatic tension lies in dialogue, not in a self-centered monologue.

The stage also becomes a partner. Everything must have its proper place, a precise position within the whole set. Diagonal, frontal and parallel arrangements each express a different quality. It cannot be left to chance whether an actor enters from the right or the left, or in which direction he turns. Similarly, each action, each mood and each movement have their own time span. The duration, speed and dynamics of time in turn affect the nature of external and internal situations. This is an unexpected experience. In dramatics the adolescent thus obtains objective criteria for his own conditions and is offered an opportunity of release in acting.

Adolescents, particularly at the age of 16 to 18, are eminently theatrical. Large themes dealing with profound, crucial problems, with poignant images and real, sometimes drastically realistic happenings revealing the heights and depths of human nature and of social and spiritual background, appeal to them most strongly. That is why Shakespeare and Schiller are especially suitable, and among more recent authors Hauptmann, Hebbel, Ostrowski or 20th century playwrights such as Gorki, Brecht and Frisch.

c) Implications of dramatic performances

In December 1975, Grade 10a performed "Der Wald" (The Forest) by Ostrowski. Much time had been spent in selecting a suitable play. It was to be a comedy. Many suggestions were made, but after initial enthusiasm the pupils realized that they needed to follow certain criteria; for instance, the cast had to be large enough to offer a part to as many pupils as possible. It did not matter if the roles were difficult; at their age the pupils should be able to cope with them. Finally, "Der Wald" by Ostrowski was chosen. This decision was partly influenced by the fact that the class had acquired an understanding of Russian emotionality in their Russian language lessons.

When the date of the performance had been set, three teachers took charge of the rehearsals. Ten boys were assigned to attend to the stage-work and lighting. Parents were roped in to procure stage furniture, costumes and other requisites. Borrowed costumes were altered by mothers and girl pupils under the supervision of the needlework teacher.

Stage setters and lighting operators worked on the sets when the stage was not needed for rehearsal. Somehow they procured laths, paint, plaster and fabrics. After several attempts a backdrop of a forest with coloured light and shadow began to take shape. Three huge trees, their tops disappearing into the ceiling, stood in front. Their trunks and branches had been built of laths and wire covered with fabric and painted. They had to be solid enough to be carried on and off the stage.

The first wave of enthusiasm was utilized for intensive rehearsing. Each character had to be true to type in appearance, speech and movement. The main work was done from 3 to 8 p.m. Most participants even gave up their autumn holiday, rehearsing from 8 a.m. to noon, learning their parts in the afternoons and meeting in the evenings at pizza parties to enjoy an "artists' atmosphere". None of this would have been possible during term-time.

Some had to work hard to put life into their performance. One boy, however, hit it off straightaway. But he rested on his laurels and neglected to learn his part. A few days before the performance his acting was excellent but he still did not know his lines. It was a lesson to all that the best acting is useless if the text has not been learnt. Another pupil had chosen the part of an old servant who sees through the weaknesses of the people around him. In trying to move and speak in character he discovered that the role he had selected was entirely alien to his own nature, and he strongly objected to transforming his whole being to fit the part. At the next rehearsal he made a half-hearted attempt, caricaturing the servant's speech and making his classmates laugh. But suddenly, the role character was there, in the round. He lived the part.

Through such surprising successes the pupils got to know new aspects of their own and their classmates' natures. They enjoyed changing the image they had had of themselves and of the others. Eager to prove that they had many hidden capacities, they tried to push their versatility to the very limit, and only the fact that they had come to know each other extremely well in the many years spent together in the class community prevented them from overstepping this limit. The stability of the group enables each pupil to try out various roles without the risk of being identified with them by his classmates. This practice in laying themselves open to doubt and proving themselves capable of assuming some of these roles is an important preparation for social learning.

Excitement reaches a climax in the actual performances. The stage fright, the trembling, the wish to be swallowed up by the earth, the compulsion to make one's entrance, to stand in the limelight, and then the almost overpowering impact of the wave of attention rising up from the 500 spectators! But one must pull oneself together, and suddenly one regains one's balance, one *is* one's role.

Several performances were given for pupils and parents. But the most rewarding was a performance in the juvenile prison. These prisoners were especially grateful that the visitors had not come to inspect them but to offer them something. In the conversation after the performance an almost cordial atmosphere developed spontaneously. The contacts then established were maintained and gave the pupils insights into a world that had been virtually unknown to them. Eventually a pupil-prisoner contact group was formed which met once a week in the prison for joint artistic activities.

d) Dramatics as a project

All the arts are needed for school dramatics, as are the pupils' skills in craft work without which it would be impossible to undertake such large-scale activities. In fact, during the period of preparing a theatrical performance most lessons are largely focussed on this purpose:

- Eurhythmy, the basis of all art of movement, has already developed in the pupils a certain conscious use of their motor ability.

- Music and elocution lay the foundations for speaking on the stage. When a performance of Hofmannsthal's "Jedermann" (Everyman) was prepared, the music teacher, who had composed his own music for the play, rehearsed the polyphonic and solo parts and the dancing songs with the whole class.

- Painting and drawing lessons stimulate the pupils

to translate selected scenes into colour and line. Later the class makes the large posters for the performance in the form of woodcuts or linocuts, watercolour paintings or ink drawing.

- In modelling lessons models of the stage sets and of individual parts are produced, to be built subsequently in the workshops with the instructor's help.
- In the toymaking lessons, the pupils make figurines representing characters in the play. They also design costumes and stage decoration.
- In the needlework lessons they produce costumes and pieces of decoration.
- In social studies, the theory of temperaments is illustrated by characters in the play, and role-behaviour is discussed in the context of social behaviour.
- In the poetry block period, analysis of the structure of works of arts helps the pupils to recognize the structural laws governing the play.

Johannes Matthiessen, Georg Rist, Wolfgang Veit

## 2.5 Grade 11

### 2.5.1 *Learning in the social domain*

The adult world interests a 16 year old mostly insofar as it enables him to acquire factual competence. His attitude to social conditions and conventions tends to be one of opposition. He tries to rebel against or experiment with them, with the result that he is regarded as a lout. But what he is really searching for is models to guide, inspire and also correct him.

At the age of 17 or 18, his interest begins to turn towards the social domain of human relationships, for which he often shows a special gift and into which he desires to integrate. Hence the entire 11th school year is dominated by the motif of learning in the social field. This helps the adolescent on the way to finding his identity. The foundation of specialized competence he has built up in the tenth grade is extended and raised to a higher level by new task areas.

In the training periods in industrial enterprises, in electrical engineering and fitting workshops, he must be able to hold his own among adult co-workers. He experiences how his role in the working group depends on the quality of his work and on his attitude to it. The training periods in kindergarten and hospital demand empathy and spontaneous action to meet specific, even exceptional situations, such as assistance in emergencies at the hospital or independent charge of a kindergarten group.

One pupil writes in his report:

"The fact that the kindergarten teacher invested me with wide, sometimes almost too wide responsibilities has given me much food for thought. I am still not certain whether this is a good or a bad thing. When I have full responsibility for the group the children feel that my word counts. If I had no responsibility they would not regard me as a person of authority. But even when I have been given responsibility it depends on my behaviour whether or not they accept my authority."

Since the situations are never artificial or simulated but always real, such responsibility becomes the decisive learning motivation. This kind of learning in the social domain trains will-power and teaches purposeful, responsible behaviour.

In addition to these pedagogical considerations, the school's decision to hold officially recognized examinations on completion of Grades 12, 13 and 14 determines the structure of the curriculum from Grade 11 upwards, as shown in Figure 8.

As the practical kindergarten and hospital training can only be given in the mornings, and this timing also has certain advantages for industrial training, the academic lessons are held in the afternoons. The timetable for Grades 11 and 12 is shown in Figure 9.

## School Structure from Grade 11 to Grade 14.
### Career Choices and Examinations

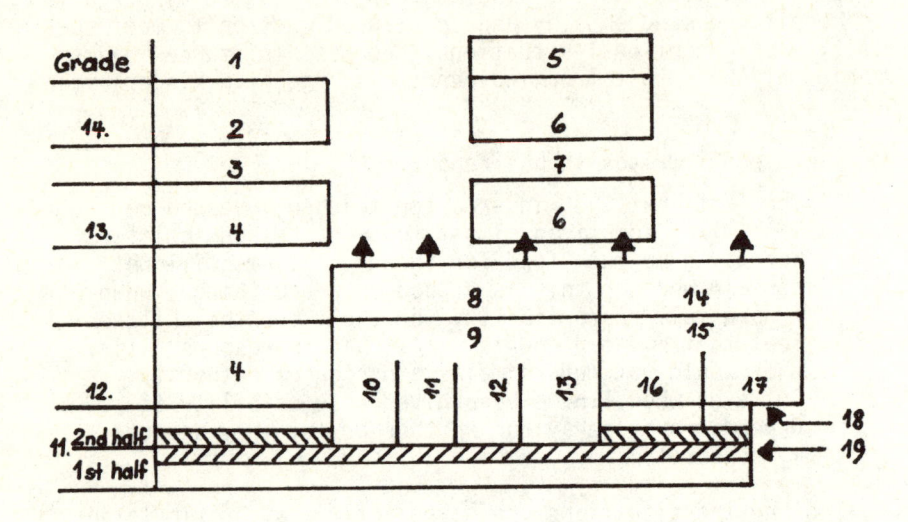

Intermediate Secondary School Leaving Certificate entitling to entry into an advanced technical school, provisonally or definitively awarded by conference decision.

The width of the rectangulars in the sections "Specialized Workers" and "Social/Technical Section" roughly represents the percentage of pupils taking these courses in each grade.

FIGURE 8

Explanations to Figure 8:

1) Colloquy re certification as qualified pre-school teacher and entitlement to entry into Colleges of Techology or Social Work
2) Probation year directed by the School
3) Pre-school teacher examination
4) Pre-school teacher

5) Final secondary education certificate entitling to University entrance
6) General Studies Section
7) Selective promotion
8) Skilled workers (apprenticeship) examination, with or without certificate entitling to entry into an advanced technical school
9) Specialized Workers Section
10) Dressmaker
11) Joiner
12) Electrician
13) Metal Workers: Machine Fitter, Mechanic, Lathe Turner
14) Qualification for entry into College of Technology or College for Social Work
15) Social/Technical Section
16) Social
17) Technical
18) After completion of Specialized Workers Section
19) Choice of career area. The pupil chooses one of the following occupational areas, in which he wants to obtain a diploma:

- Pre-school teaching / social work
- Woodwork (joinery)
- Metal (machine fitter, mechanic, turner)
- Electrical engineering (electrician)
- Textiles (tailor, dressmaker).

After this decision he cannot change over to a different area until he has passed the relevant examination. The original conception of Hibernia School education did not envisage specialization leading to a certificate of apprenticeship or state diploma at this stage. The pupils would have left the school equipped with a broad knowledge of several occupational areas (metal, wood, electricity, etc.) and would have specialized in a particular occupation at their place of work.

Further explanations to Figure 8:

- After passing the examination, a prospective pre-school teacher may change over to the General Studies Section or the Social Work/ Technical Section either before or after doing his probation year.

- Alternatively, a pupil who has passed the examination entitling to entry into a College of Technology (Social Work) may enter the 13th grade of pre-school teacher education.

- In contrast to the general practice at the Hibernia School, promotion from Grade 13 to Grade 14 of the General Studies Section is not automatic but selective.

- The late date of the career decisions (choice of occupational area comes halfway through Grade 11 and, in particular, decision on whether or not to go in for further or higher education at the end of Grade 12) makes it possible for future doctors and lawyers, mechanics and pre-school teachers, to have joint social experiences within the same class. For the individual pupil this late date means that he can take his decision on the basis of personal experience in a variety of occupational areas and of knowledge of his learning ability in the academic subjects. 17 and 18 1/2 years respectively are appropriate ages for making these decisions.

105

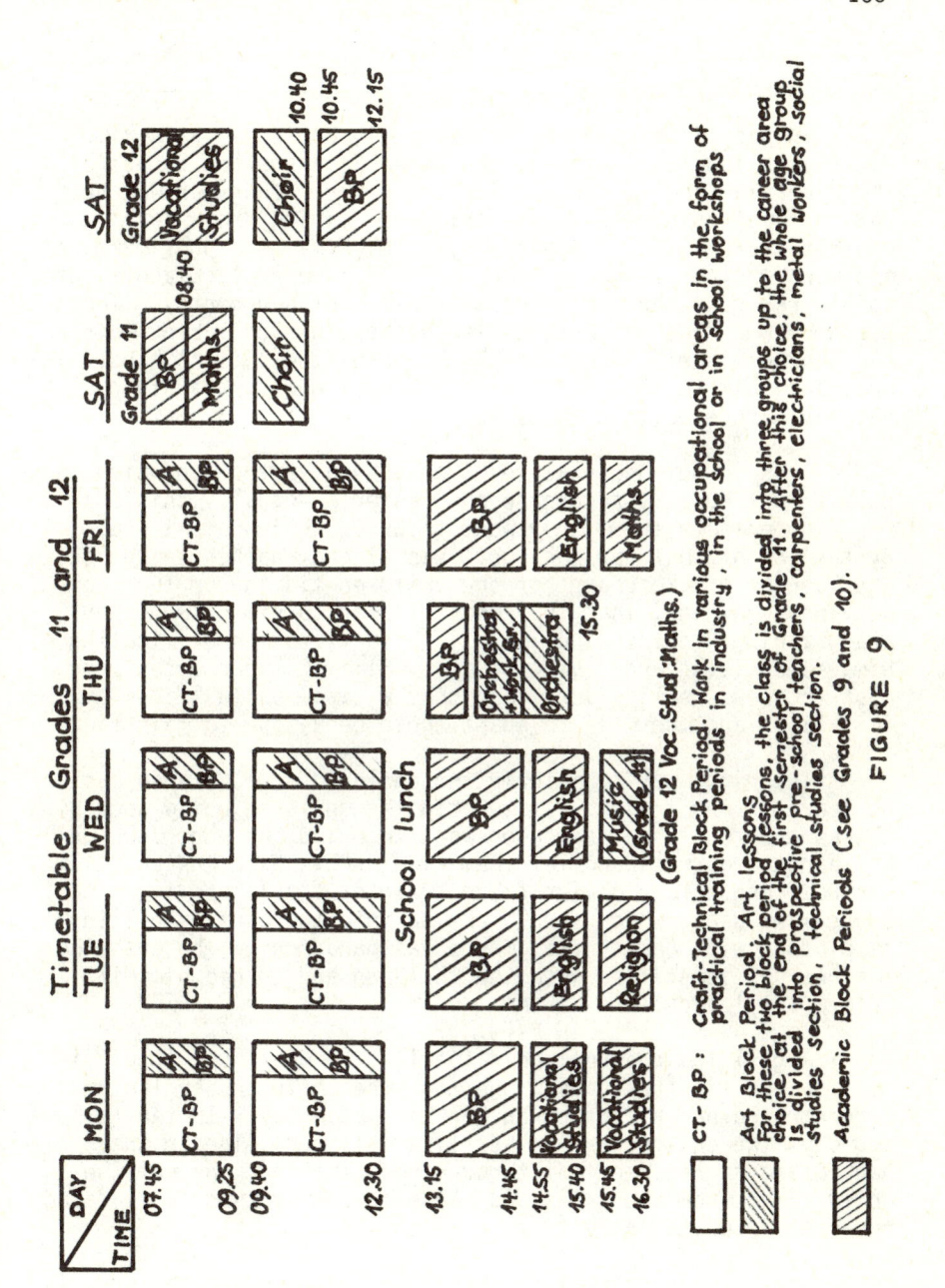

FIGURE 9

## 2.5.2 *Practical period in the kindergarten as part of social development*

In the first semester of Grade 11, one pupil at a time works as a trainee in one of the three kindergarten groups of the Hibernia School. On his first day, one young man watches, rather helplessly, the little children washing their dolls' clothes, for this is "laundry day". Clearly he cannot make up his mind whether to join in or not. Four-year old Claudia comes to his rescue. She has to go to the toilet - urgently. The teacher, who does not want to leave the other children, says: "Go and help her!" Hesitatingly he takes the child's hand. It occurs to him to say: "You're a big girl now!" Claudia nods happily, and everything goes well.

This is but one example of an unusual situation which the pupils must quickly recognize and master. Actually this challenge appeals to them, they want to prove their competence. By the end of that day the pupil has already gained enough self-confidence to take charge of the children tidying up the room. He finds, however, that they won't listen to him. "But they are watching," the teacher says. In fact, some are imitating him, supervising and giving orders. Similar experiences make most trainees realize very soon that a small child learns by imitation, and they try to adapt their behaviour to this fact.

The right way to join in the children's games also has to be learnt. One trainee was to help the children build something. But as they could not agree on what to build, he went down on his hands and knees and let them ride on his back instead. It was not long before children and trainee were locked in a struggling heap, which then broke up into two parties pelting each other with chestnuts. There was pandemonium, because the trainee had identified with the children and turned himself into a little boy.

A girl trainee noticed a little girl who found it difficult to join in the games. She took the child on her lap and concentrated her attention on her the whole day. In the following days the child clung to her like a limpet. The trainee had failed to realize that through her behaviour she set the child apart from the group and hindered rather than facilitated her access to its activities.

A good means of establishing contact with the children is role-playing at the start of the kindergarten day. The children are allowed to play with all the furnishings, to build ships, aeroplanes, cars, cranes, farmhouses out of tables, chairs, benches, bricks, rugs and cushions. They also dress up for these games. The trainees help them in building, they may also join in the play. Many find it difficult to enter the children's imaginary world, and their inadequate contact and lack of understanding is mirrored in the children's behaviour. For instance, the children are building an expedition truck. The trainee wants to be a lion whom the children are to catch and put in the truck. But when it comes to the catching stage he irritates them by evading them persistently. He is enjoying that game, but it soon degenerates into a riot. The children say: "He is silly, he is not a real lion, he has spoilt the whole play." They turn their backs on him and play on alone. Then the pupil realizes that he has not taken the children's play seriously enough. By acting according to his own rather than their ideas he has upset their fantasy world.

Thus the trainees gain psychological insight from experience. They learn to observe, control and improve themselves. Talks with the teacher, who points out the effects their attitude to the children has on individuals and on the whole group, are of great assistance. In playing with the children the boys must learn to find their role as adults, while many of the girls are already too grown up and must make a greater effort to establish direct contact. Eventually, their daily work with the kindergarten group gives the trainees the self-assurance they need to participate in the children's play while guiding it towards educational goals by means suited to the situation.

The children have decided to build a ship. The trainee helps them to pile up tables. Now and then he makes a suggestion for improving the ship, but always withdraws again and lets the children continue by themselves. They then assign the roles. Naturally, they choose the trainee to be captain. But he does not accept the role. He hands it over to a shy, reserved little boy whom the children would not have chosen. He himself wants to be third officer. As such he guides the play without the children being aware of it. He tells the shy captain what to do to make the others obey his orders. The cheekiest of the boys is sent down to the hull to check whether the hatches are closed and everything is in good order. A girl becomes radio operator, others are cooks, divers, deckhands, passengers, ship's sirens, or just people dangling their feet in the water. The children are so entirely immersed in the game that they call out to the passing teacher: "Look out, you'll drown! You can't walk across the sea!" This pupil has done his job well. He has taken the game seriously, has entered into the children's fantasy world and yet guarded the detachment necessary to guide them.

If the 17 year olds' desire for meaningful activity in the social domain is to be fulfilled, they must learn to perceive a situation and themselves in it. The informal, natural and at the same time merciless demands of kindergarten work teach them to do so. This is an excellent help towards self-knowledge and self-education. Many pupils start off lightheartedly playing with the children. But they easily lose control. The children unerringly find their weak points. They trip them up, or a whole crowd pulls them down to the floor and sits on them triumphantly. To become fruitful, the various types of situation must be experienced repeatedly. In the following year a single incident is then often sufficient for the trainee to comprehend why and where he has gone wrong.

Dagmar Siefer and Peter Schneider

2.5.3 *Work in a hospital*

Before the pupils decide on their career area in which they want to specialize, they undergo a period of practical work in one of the nearby hospitals. In the Vocational Study lessons they have learnt about the social structure of a hospital, the roles of doctors, nursing personnel and patients. Now they will see all this from the inside and have an opportunity of proving their competence and understanding.

In the autumn of 1976 pupils from Grade 11a and 11b turned up on the first day of their hospital period full of sympathy for the poor patients and eager to help them, but were immediately brought down to earth: "Where is your overall? Go home and get it. And take your nail-varnish off." On the next day they were taken to a ward and the sister informed them of their duties. Their experiences are described in the reports below.

a) Grade 11 pupils' reports on their hospital work, 1976

My duties were to relieve the nursing personnel of some of their routine work, such as going to the pharmacy to fetch the medicines that had been ordered and arrange them in the medicine cabinet. I was shown all the important departments - laboratory, X-ray, sterilization and surgery department and pharmacy. Then I had to take the patients to the various places outside the ward, the majority to the X-ray and electrocardiogram rooms. I also had to take off bedsheets, wash and disinfect them and remake the beds. Every morning I distributed thermometers to the patients, re-collected them after a few minutes and entered the patients' temperature and pulse rate on the charts. In some cases I had to measure the urine every morning. Another of my duties was to help some patients get out of and into bed. An old man had to be fed regularly, and every other day I had to shave him. Towards the end of the training period I was entrusted with tasks such as reading and entering blood counts and flushing out bladders.

My most interesting experience I owe to the ward doctor, who allowed me to watch a bowel test and a liver test, for which an instrument must be introduced into the abdomen. Materially much is being done for the patients. They get the best rest, food and treatment. What is lacking in my opinion is human contact between personnel and patient, though this varies with the personality of the nurses. I think that nursing is a very interesting profession. I liked my work, because I learnt something of which I had no previous knowledge or experience. But it seems to me that three weeks' practice is too short. One had just begun to get to know the work and make contact with the patients when it was all over.

Christoph Dumpe, Grade 11a

At 6 a.m. I started my practical period in an infants ward. My field of duty comprised the babies' room, the mothers' room and the kitchen. First we fed the babies. The most important thing is to support their heads so that they do not fall back. A rubber sheet is placed under the babies' bodies because they are usually wet. I also put a nappy under the baby's chin. Some spit when drinking, others do not. In the first three days every baby gets the bottle because the mothers do not yet have milk. In feeding the babies I must take care that the hole in the nipple is on top, that the milk is not too hot, and that I do not accidentally block the child's nose with the nipple. When it has drunk enough I wait until it has burped, which indicates that the stomach has absorbed the food. After that a baby rarely spits it out. After the feeding we usually change the nappies (one medium and one thin layer for the day or one thick, one medium and one thin layer for the night). Then we take turns in cleaning and sterilizing the bottles and preparing fresh ones for the 10 o'clock feed.

Dagmar Harder, Grade 11b

The expectations with which I started the practice period were only partially fulfilled. The introduction to the work was very brief, but this is justified because one cannot remember everything at once.

I particularly disliked the constant rush in my ward. I was always being urged to work more swiftly. Of course I realize that in a ward the work must be done rather faster than might be desirable, but why should I rush only to hang around afterwards? Just because the nurse is nervous because the sister is ill? It happened not infrequently that in our haste to roll the cots into the bathing room we knocked them so hard against the door frame that the babies got a shock and started screaming. Things like that should not happen, for those tiny beings are particularly sensitive to jolts. This is very obvious when their nappies are changed. If I turn the baby over too often or too rapidly it immediately starts vomiting. If I am too hasty or too rough when putting its little arms into the jacket it screams. But if I remain calm despite the hurry and endeavour to do all these things gently though swiftly with a practised hand, the baby stays quiet. It may even go on sleeping while I handle it.

Elisabeth Kussmaul, Grade 11b

I should like to compare my experiences as a hospital trainee with those I had as a patient in 1971. When I was a patient the nurses' work did not seem to me to be very strenuous. I only saw them waking the patients, making the beds and distributing the meals. Every other day they took the patients' temperatures. The amount of work they had to do did not appear heavy. Now I know how much time it takes to make the beds and distribute the meals if one has to look after 4 to 5 rooms. In addition there is the nursing of bed-ridden patients - there had been none in my room - who must be washed and fed and whose beds must be made. If such a patient weighs 15 stone, washing him and making his bed can be a back-breaking job. And besides these nursing duties the usual routine work has to be done.

When I was a patient I was very amused by a little boy who rang for the nurse every ten minutes. As a trainee I found it annoying if patients kept ringing for me for trivial reasons while I was busy elsewhere.

Martin Paweletz, Grade 11a

The pupils work in the hospital for four hours per day, either from 6 to 10 o'clock or from 8 to 12. Then they go back to school for lunch. The afternoon block periods and regular lessons are also geared to the respective training periods. There is a lively exchange of impressions and experiences. Comparisons are made and questions discussed, such as:

- Is the rough manner of some nurses justified?
- Should one tell a terminally ill patient that he is going to die?
- Should one inform an incurably ill patient of his condition?
- Have doctors got a right to prolong artificially a life of intense suffering?

The seriousness of questions such as these suggests that many pupils are profoundly touched by their experiences. Some of them work voluntarily in their wards at weekends.

This training period confronts the pupils with a reality that had been almost entirely unknown to them. Many consciously experience their active participation in this reality, the shouldering of a responsibility which frightens them at first, as the beginning of adulthood. Nearly all of them consider it right and beneficial that everyone, regardless of his future occupation, should get to know, through active involvement, this domain of illness, birth and death which he will perforce have to go through in his later life.

Peter Schneider and Gisela Klonk

## 2.5.4 *Practical experience in a large-scale chemical plant*

In the central workshop of the VEBA chemical plant a pupil has been tracing the centre points of 35 holes to be drilled on a piece of steel tubing some 250 mm in diameter and 1.2 m in length. When he has finished he studies first the blueprint, then the lines and crosspoints he has traced on the hard special alloy steel and is relieved to find that everything seems all right. But suddenly he is overcome by a strange new feeling: if he has made a mistake and the holes are drilled where he has indicated, material worth DM 6,000 will have to be scrapped! The skilled worker in charge of him is busy doing piece work in the drilling shop. The pupil is supposed to do his tracing and centering independently. And after all, why should he not work independently like the other adults? Again he checks with the utmost concentration. Everything is correct. But after a moment's relief, the doubts return, and he checks for the third time. As he still finds no mistake, he seizes hammer and centre punch, centres the drillholes and takes the steel tube to the drilling shop.

The first three weeks of his training period pass quickly. He is impressed by the time clock. His check-in card shows that he has never been late. When the work situation permits, the pupil often talks with the skilled worker to whom he is attached, and who has a son of exactly the same age. In these conversations they discuss many technical details, as well as the works council and working conditions in general. Much can also be explained by the workshop teacher from the School who supervises the pupils' training and assigns each one to a skilled worker.

In the next three weeks this same trainee helps to install an automatic remote control system. A control room twice the size of a classroom is to be set up which will signal information on temperature, pressure, chemical composition, etc. A number of measuring and recording instruments register the measurements and emit electrical impulses which adjust valves on the boilers. Like the other electricians, the trainee crawls through the metal casings wiring the instruments under the supervision of his new senior. To start with, he only does what he is told to do, applying the skills and knowledge he has acquired in the electrical block periods at school. But after a few days he begins to understand parts of the intricate system. Again his senior, an ex-Hibernia School pupil, tells him about the works council, works meetings, calculation and management and explains the electrical control system.

The final three weeks of his training period are spent in the quality control department. This room is much quieter than the others. Measuring instruments are repaired there and recalibrated so as to be absolutely precise and reliable. The trainee notices that his status rises with the accuracy and steadiness of his work. Not every pupil in Grade 11 is equally successful.

Berthold May


2.5.5 *Study of Parzival in Grade 11*

In Grade 11 with its practical training periods in which

the pupils, individually or in small groups, test their competence in practical work and gain first-hand knowledge of economic-technical as well as social relationships, an afternoon block period in German literature focusses on the theme of Parzival. In the treatment of this subject the literary and language aspects take second place to its study as an exemplar of human life.

The text is read in a prose version; only specially poignant parts are recited in the original form, i.e. in middle high German verse. This arrangement makes for an understanding of the historical situation, while not neglecting the literary aspect.

Parzival's extraordinary life story raises many moral issues the pupils eagerly discuss. His excessively sheltered upbringing by his widowed mother leaves him entirely innocent, without any knowledge of the sinful world. But man's innate urge to find his own identity drives him to leave his mother and join a group of errant knights. Unknown to him she dies of grief. He is thus guilty of having innocently caused her death. This problem of becoming guilty as a result of an action which appeared necessary profoundly exercises the pupils' minds.

Parzival knows neither his name nor his origin. His identity is gradually revealed to him in encounters with Sigune, a symbolic figure in the story, whom he meets every time he has taken a major step in his development, when he has made a social experience. Finding one's own identity thus depends on such existential experiences. This is another problem the pupils seize upon at once. How does one recognize one's real self? Moments in which they recognized themselves for the first time as individuals different from others surge up in the pupils' memories and lead to the insight that men discover their identity through contact with other people.

By innocently following his mother's simple teachings in a world in which behaviour is regulated by firm rules, Parzival incurs misfortune and serious guilt. He finds a guide, the knight Gurnemanz, who teaches him the knightly virtue of helping the weak. But he is still not equipped to meet higher demands. When his mysterious fate leads him to the castle of the holy grail and he applies the virtue of tactful silence he has recently learnt from Gurnemanz, he fails the test of true humanity and is sent away in derision. This episode agitates the pupils. As it is extremely difficult to imagine a degree of maturity far beyond one's age, they cannot understand why Parzival should be punished for a mistake they themselves would have made. Again it is a problem of guilt innocently incurred. The scene becomes comprehensible only in reviewing the whole of Parzival's life, which is characterized by the fact that he repeatedly becomes guilty through inexperience and ignorance, but finds and seizes opportunities of atoning for the wrong he has done. From this insight the pupils deduce that, while an individual may be confronted with his goal in life at an early age, he must be prepared and mature enough to recognize and reach it.

The relationship between man and woman is exemplified by the experience of Parzival's friend, the knight Gawan, who has three encounters with women representing three stages in the development of this relationship. Gawan meets the personification of evil in Klingsor's realm. That Gawan and Parzival must be seen as one person becomes clear later when they recognize each other as they are about to fight a duel.

Eventually Parzival returns to the castle of the holy grail, passes the test and is made king of the grail. He is then reunited with his wife and sons, an indication that the high task to which he has been called does not alienate him from the world but is a part of every human life.

Specially interested pupils like to read in the school library Chrétien de Troyes' "Perceval", the source from which Wolfram von Eschenbach took the Parzival story. They then report on what they have read, and often the whole class goes to the library to compare the two texts.

German lessons are particularly suitable for initiating pupils into the world of books and the use of reference works. The library is open to both pupils and teachers during the whole school day, and everybody makes his own entries for taking out and returning books. Many upper grade pupils spend their leisure time or work together there. This is a good preparation for their future use of public libraries; it also reflects the Parzival theme: becoming independent, knowing one's way about and entering new territory.

Bertram Berg

## 2.6 Grade 12

### 2.6.1 *Preparation for maturity*

Three considerations govern the curriculum for Grade 12:
- Specialized education has reached the stage where work can be done with an overview of its wider context.
- The sense of social responsibility expands to include responsibility for joint tasks.
- The new ability to comprehend wider inter-connections arouses the pupils' interest in complex overviews.

The structure of industrial and social organization, capital and its driving forces, the infinite in mathematics and the individuality expressed in a portrait lead to an existential approach to problems and give an inkling of dimensions far exceeding experience. In grappling with such problems the adolescents search for a philosophy of life into which their experiences and insights can be meaningfully fitted.

The four examples given below may show how the methods and contents of education are designed to take account of these aspects, the validity of which has been confirmed by many years of experience:

1) Future electricians have full responsibility for wiring a house. At the same time they act as foremen to Grade 11 pupils. Despite time pressure their work must be reliable.

2) In Economics, the knowledge the pupils have accumulated of various work processes, from the forestry period via school work-shops, kindergarten, hospital to industrial plant, provides the basis for purposeful exploration of a selected organization. An enterprise or institution is now studied as a whole in all its aspects: production, work organization, marketing, personnel management and sociology of work. These studies of a single enterprise or institution then lead to a consideration of national and world-wide interconnections and constraints.

3) In art lessons the pupils do a complete piece of work, a portrait head, generally a kind of self-portrait, based on perception of their own heads and accurate observation. They usually take it home as proud testimony of their artistic work at school.

4) The clearest evidence of competence is, however, a successful piece of work made in order to qualify as a skilled craftsman. It shows that the pupil has learnt to apply the abilities and skills he has acquired with circumspection and independence.

## 2.6.2 *The training of pre-school teachers*

Throughout the practical kindergarten periods (8 weeks in Grade 11, after the career decision, 15 weeks in Grade 12, and 9 weeks in Grade 13) one aim is to develop the trainees' powers of observation. Their psychological, educational and sociological ideas are to be concretized by means of exact, differentiated observation.

The following report on a Grade 12 student may show that this observation does not merely consist in leisurely looking-on but involves alert action:

On a Monday morning Uta's task is to practise "wet-in-wet" painting with a group of children. In this technique a large sheet of paper is soaked in water, then placed on a painting board and smoothed out with a damp sponge. The three basic colours red, yellow and blue are then applied to large areas with a broad brush. The outlines get a little blurred, but this makes the colours, of which the children have individual likes and dislikes, all the more effective.

On the preceding Monday, when Uta was given this task for the first time, she had underestimated the accidents that may happen when there are 10 jars of water and 30 paint bowls on the table. One jar of water had been knocked over because she had not seated the children at sufficient distance from each other, and one of their "works of art" had been soaked, to a flood of tears. Some children did not wash out the brush before dipping it into another colour, and soon a number of bowls contained only mixed colours. With all these misadventures Uta, a good painter who had looked forward to giving advice on the actual painting, had had no time to do so.

As usual on a Monday, the children had come to the kindergarten full of the Sunday's experiences. "Bang, bang, bang, I'll shoot you dead" - one boy played a robber. "Boo, boo - I am Dracula" - another imitated a television monster. All tended to quarrel and fight more than they did on other days of the week. Painting was meant to bring these imposed impressions under control.

After this experience Uta had carefully thought out her procedure. Three children helped her setting out the jars of water, bowls of paint and painting boards at suitable distances on the table. Then she fetched the others in from the playground, made them sing a song about a flag fluttering in the wind, stretch up their arms and mime the flag's movement with their hands. Nobody dipped his hand into the water or paint bowls. Then the brushes were distributed, and after another song to which the brushes were waved in the air the painting started. Uta kept an eye on the whole group to make sure that the brushes were washed before each colour change while she went round giving advice. After 15 minutes each child had painted at least one picture - a house, a lake, the sun, a ship or something undefinable.

In painting with a kindergarten group a trainee must be capable of watching all of them and of reacting pedagogically as the situation demands. If for a moment she merely looks on or thinks of herself, some mishap is bound to occur. At this stage the trainees must learn to act with presence of mind on the basis of differentiated observation. In the subsequent theoretical kindergarten block period, these observations serve as starting points for studying the behaviour of individual children. Connections are sought between the children's physique, habits and temperaments. For instance, is there a relationship between timid, inhibited behaviour and paleness or thin bone structure? What are the eating habits of the various temperaments? Does a psychologically well-balanced child tend to be plump? What are the influences of nutrition? Can certain types of behaviour be limited to a definite age? Towards the end of the block period the criteria that have been found are arranged in a sequence, starting with physical build, skin colour and other external characteristics and ending with psychological reactions. Each trainee then has to observe one child from the viewpoint of these criteria in the subsequent six week period and submit a report, in which she also tries to identify the developmental stage of the child concerned and describes the educational measures she has taken to further it.

In Grade 13 the study of the children's individual characters is extended to the adult in charge of them, including themselves, and his effect upon them. This helps them to control their own temperaments.

In this way the training of pre-school teachers aims to develop educational concepts based on what is observable. The experiences gathered in the practical social periods in Grade 11 prepare the ground for more conscious use of such fundamental abilities. Learning to observe accurately and with differentiation, to distinguish critically between the capacities of the various senses and to be critical vis-à-vis their own judgements is appropriate for 17-18 year olds because observation and disciplined, conscious judgement are essential for responsible activity in the social domain. In this training also the learning contents, methods and settings are thus related to the pupils' age and built upon earlier learning (painting, needlework, toy-making, etc.).

Gisela Klonk

2.6.3 *Electrical installation*

The electrical workshop accepts orders for installation work. Grade 12 students, now training to become electricians, submit tenders for public orders.

When an order has been received, it is discussed by the group which is to execute it on the basis of the building blueprints, and the group then often inspects the site together with the owner or the architect. It is important for their commitment to the job that they should make the acquaintance of both. They listen to conversations about special wishes and the cost of meeting them, they see how compromises are arrived at. Then the work schedules and calculations are worked out. Not infrequently the time estimates are over-optimistic.

Once the installation work starts the pupils are obliged to fit in with the overall construction schedule. Certain insulation cables must be laid immediately before the concrete is poured. Exceeding the deadline entails costly additional work. Other cables have to be put in prior to the plastering. At the beginning it often becomes painfully evident that the time schedule made no allowance for bad weather. Then the electricians wait sullenly until the roof is ready, or even until the heating functions. In between plastering and wallpapering the wire circuits and the switches must be put in. When at last all these jobs have been done and a test has confirmed that the whole electrical system is functioning well, the group heaves a sigh of relief.

Specialized skill, a brisk working pace and reliability are indispensable in all these tasks. The social structure of the group rests on these characteristics and on the degree of cooperation and readiness within the group to correct faults. Sick leave is viewed from a new perspective: "Will they be able to manage without me? Am I really so ill that I cannot go to work?" Rightly the pupils say: "On the building site a group becomes a genuine team."

For educational reasons the work process is divided up. Jobs requiring a high degree of specialized knowledge and skill are allocated to Grade 12 boys and girls, who are capable of working independently. They act as a kind of foremen to the pupils of Grade 11 who should learn from them.

The tenants or the owner frequently interrupt the work with special requests. They want wall plugs or lighting arrangements, television or telephone connections to be changed, and all this has to be done before the painters start work. Nevertheless each trainee is responsible for his job. He must test it as severely as will the authorities when the whole installation is finished, and this implies knowing and observing the relevant regulations.

Talks with the other workmen on the site, who treat the trainees as almost equal partners in a common working situation, are another feature of this training period.

Friedrich Pfannenschmidt

## 2.6.4 *Economic studies*

A future electrician is giving a talk. His group has tendered for the electrical installation in a house but did not get the order because a competitor submitted a cheaper offer. "You probably included the smoking break in your calculation," says a wit from the metal group. This group has seen in its training period in a large concern how precisely all individual operations are calculated in piece-work. In the discussion the concept of profitability emerges. Exact calculation of working time is necessary to achieve profitability. One student who had talked a lot with the workers and the foreman in his factory says: "If an enterprise does not operate profitably, it will be closed and everybody will be sacked. That is why they must save material, avoid scrap, etc. No business can in the long run spend more than it earns." A girl says: "Piece-work is just a means of increasing the owner's profit." "But the workers' council which represents the interests of the workers has agreed," is a reply. "No, the workers' council has no say in that." Who is right? The relevant legislation, "Workers' Participation in Fixing the Rates for Piece-Work and Bonuses", is consulted.

Many questions come up in the discussion. Why do white collar workers get a fixed salary whereas manual workers are paid by output? Why do the qualified workers not make their own work schedules and calculations? The concept of alienation crops up. An unskilled labourer only does parts, in many cases a minute fraction, of the whole production process; but does a qualified chemical worker controlling a fully automatic plant know what is being produced?

Another subject of discussion is workers' participation. How must a factory be organized and structured to enable every worker to participate? Do such factories exist? While the pupils know something about workers' participation in the operational field from their own experience, workers' participation in management has to be dealt with in the Economic Studies lessons. The firm in which the pupils do their training is taken as an example. Its legal status is that of a joint stock company. This means that there are capital owners, a Board of Management and the work force. Both sides are represented on the Board of Directors.

After a discussion on "What is capital?" and "What are its functions?", a study of the overall structure of the enterprise reveals the significance of capital ownership. The question arises to what extent capital should be at the owner's free disposal.

The main objective of Economic Studies is to raise to the level of conscious thought, analysis and conceptualization the impressions and experiences the students have gained in their varied practical work - manual and machine work, division of labour, calculation. In Grade 12 they are introduced to wider contexts so as to obtain a certain overview. In these lessons it is not only the present state of affairs that is of interest, but also how they feel things "should be". They formulate problems concerning human dignity and democratization of the workplace, and whether high output could not also be achieved through working groups organizing themselves and being responsible to themselves. After two weeks of preparation the whole class travels to another town to explore an industrial enterprise. For a week they live in a youth hostel and participate in the morning shifts in the selected factory, which may be a modern textile mill or a pencil factory or some other industrial works. The boys and girls are distributed over the various departments, where they are assigned to specific workers from Monday to Friday in order to experience in practice the social and administrative organization of the kind of work they are to study. This gives them an opportunity to question the workers. In the afternoons the personnel manager, or the head of the buying, sales or work-preparation department gives them a talk in the canteen or a lecture hall. Or they have a discussion with the works council, or the factory owner or a member of the Board of Management informs them of the company's broad lines of policy.

Often the discussions become agitated, and the teacher has to mediate between the young people's bold, "revolutionary" ideas and the viewpoints of the practitioners. The students feel very strongly about the human aspects they have discovered in working together with older, experienced factory workers, especially the monotony of the work and the workers' attitude to it. In the afternoon sessions details they know from their own industrial training periods may suddenly fall into place. For instance, they had felt that the compulsion inherent in doing piece-work in a stipulated time was degrading. But in the afternoon discussions they recognize the advantage normed timing has for exact pre- and post-calculation. The question whether exact calculation is more important than a freer, self-directed mode of working, or vice versa, often sets off a heated debate. Altogether they realize that accurate knowledge and careful observation are necessary to make feasible suggestions for change.

In the evening, the experiences of the day are set down in individual or group minutes, from which a comprehensive report is worked out later. The factory concerned receives a copy of this report, which not infrequently contains observations that are quite illuminating to the management. This is a token of our gratitude for the burden we have imposed on the enterprise. Those members who have taken part in the discussions have repeatedly stated that Hibernia students ask more concrete and pertinent questions than do those who have had no practical education.

When the outcomes of the economics block period are evaluated, in the last of the four weeks, it becomes clear that the students' concrete observations and experiences have modified their abstract and dogmatic "revolutionary" ideas. For instance, in an electrical concern most women workers were allowed to choose whether they wanted to build a complete unit, do only a small part or something in between the two. Talks with these workers showed that the vast majority preferred the mechanical type of work, i.e. doing only a small part. "Then I need not concentrate on the job but can think of my home," they said. The students took this to be an expression of total alienation. The director disagreed: it could not be called alienation because it was their own choice. In their report some pupils deduced from this situation that a fundamental change of people's attitude to work could only be achieved if the foundations for it were laid in school education. The problems of work relations that had emerged in the training periods in Grade 11 were now seen in their wider context.

In the staff conference the economics teacher came under heavy criticism from his colleagues. They could not see the need for taking the students away from school for a whole week when the time for their vocational training was already very short. The teacher had to use very potent arguments to convince them. Such disputes with the teachers and also with parents are an important characteristic of an independent school.

The economics teacher of the parallel class then reported on the experiences his class had had in a glassworks where workers' self-administration had been introduced. They had found that, while not everything appeared to function better and not all workers seemed happier, they did display more interest in the whole works and often had detailed knowledge of the economic situation of the company. The question why nevertheless only some 20 per cent were willing to take on the additional commitment of serving in self-administration bodies was discussed at length.

The fact that reformist ideas were put into practice in this company gave the pupils greater confidence in human courage and initiative. Conversations with socially aware manual and white-collar workers on new social structures within a factory are fruitful for both sides in that they offer practical ideas to the pupils and suggest solutions of their problems to the workers. Since the Hibernia School, like all Waldorf schools, also practices self-administration, such talks are in the nature of an exchange of experience.

The conference agreed that the ideas of both economics teachers should be integrated. In future, factories should be chosen in which both a highly developed work organization and principles of workers' self-administration could be studied.

Markus Kühn
Hartwig Wilken

2.6.5 *Art lessons. Modelling a human head in clay*

It has been described how in the modelling lessons of Grade 5 an animal figure is made through the gradual transformation and methodical differentiation of a simple form, a ball. The teacher so vividly described or worked out with the children the various characteristic postures of the animal concerned, from waking up and lifting its head to sniffing and moving, that they could feel the functioning of its body and transmit it to the clay. The aim was not so much to achieve a true likeness but rather to sharpen the children's eyes for characteristic movement and the interplay of the forces involved.

Modelling a human head in Grade 12 is an extension of this method. Each student has a lump of clay on his table. It is greyish brown, cold and shapeless, suggesting no potential form. The only intrinsic force it conveys is gravity. The students are aware that they are also subject to the law of gravity, but they can counteract it by employing other forces within them, they can stand upright. When they transmit this power to the clay with their hands and arms by raising it up to the shape of a column, a process constantly taking place in their own bodies becomes visible in an external object. This experience sensitizes them to similar processes in their environment, and they develop an ability to discover formative processes in nature, just as making music develops an ear for musical forms.

A mask, for instance, may be created as an expression of human inner life. It can also be made by moulding a face out of the rounded clay from pure imagination unconnected with any observation. Thus a nose may grow beyond normal human dimensions into something animal-like and grotesque.

Sculpturing a human head is intended to provide practice in experiencing formative processes, in understanding the forces involved in shaping it. For that reason the first task is a kind of self-portrait, not in front of a mirror but as an expression of inner experience, personal ideals and impulses. A hollow head is built up by setting ring upon ring of clay to form the neck, on which rings of increasing and then decreasing width are placed until a rough outline of a head is completed. An opening large enough for the hand to pass through is cut into what is going to be the back of the head. With one hand pressing from the inside, the other held against that spot on the outside, the skull and back of the head are now shaped - a lengthy process consisting entirely of feeling out the inside form and the relationship between above and below, right and left, front and back. At the same time, the ratio of the neck to the domed skull must be borne in mind. There must be a balance between support and load. The students experience the mutual conditioning of form and material. If the neck does not offer sufficient support and tensile strength, it will collapse; if the clay does not have the right consistency, i.e. if it is too wet or too dry, the same thing will happen. What is done in nature by spinal column and muscles must be achieved in the clay model by surface tension.

Already in the elementary stage the different types of head can be recognized, from long, slender or small to broad and heavy. In some the back of the head is more prominent, in others the forehead or the chin. No two heads are alike.

In the second phase of the work, attention centres on the interaction of man's inner and external world. Each rounding, each fine curve of the facial surface becomes an expression of the way in which a human being interacts with the world through his senses in breathing, seeing, hearing, smelling, tasting and speaking. The shape of the nose - straight, crooked or upturned, massive or dainty -, the position of the eyes, the curves of cheeks and chin, all express something of the sculptor's own personality, and each feature must be harmonized with the whole. The interaction of the inner with the outer world is reflected in the activity of the sculptor's hands. What one hand moulds out from the inside is taken up by the other, and vice versa. The fingertips sensitively follow each modification of the surface produced by the interaction between inside and outside.

One day a boy tells his classmates what he observed in the faces of people in the bus. The students have thus reached the stage where the exploration of their own inner self leads them to an interest in other faces. They now observe not merely people's eyes and mouths, noting whether they are in a happy or unhappy mood, but the shape of the whole head, trying to discern the character that has found expression in it.

Observation of their classmates becomes part of the lessons. The students notice that there are flat and more chiselled faces, that cheeks, eyes and mouth lie on a curvature which, when the head is turned, is visibly connected by the temple and chin areas with the back of the head. An individual's eyes, nose and mouth express the particular way in which they function. The nose, including its sides, indicates the manner in which breath is inhaled and exhaled, the mouth conveys how a person speaks and expresses emotions, such as smiling or ill-humour. Through relating every detail to the whole head, the students' attention is also drawn to less conspicuous but equally revealing features, such as forehead, temples, chin.

As a result of these studies the clay heads become more and more individualized and "alive". Sometimes one sees a student studying his "self-portrait" in deep wonder. It may not be a very good likeness, but it tells him something of his inner life. He recognizes his true nature. An artistic process has thus been completed. Through careful work, consciously carried out step by step, something of the essence of the sculptor has been embodied in the clay model which now stands as a creation in front of its creator. (4)

Eva-Maria Garbe


2.6.6 *Joint appreciation of work done in art lessons*

The art lessons do not focus on results but on the artistic process. A prominent feature is critical appreciation of the sculptures and paintings that have been produced by the students.

They react very differently to inspection of their unfinished work. Some gladly take advice from friends, talk about their intentions and accept direct help. Others permit only the teacher to assist them, and some do not even want that. In this respect they must have complete liberty. The more methodically they practised handling form and colour in the sense of Goethe's colour theory in the lower grades, the more they can be left to work on their own in Grades 11 and 12. The teaching method consists in selecting tasks that require an appropriate selection and application of material. For instance, while in Grade 12 the teacher may decide on the use of watercolours for landscapes, flowers, faces or free compositions, each student himself chooses the technique he is going to use - wet-in-wet, layer technique or a mixture of both. If the teacher is a professional painter or sculptor, the learning situation is one of free cooperation, and a student may find that the teacher understands his intention better than he does himself.

The teacher must also know that there is no intrinsic superiority in art, as there is in technical work with its defined criteria of quality. This becomes very clear when the whole group appraises an exhibition of finished work. Objectivity should be the rule. Personal likes or dislikes should not be expressed unless the teacher wants to uncover the reasons that lead to approval or rejection. Usually there are some particularly successful pieces which can provide standards for critical appreciation of the others. For instance, some paintings or sculptures may be technically satisfactory but lack tension or balance; colours may be bereft of their special effect by being too firmly compressed into drawn outlines. Similar criteria apply to the degree to which form-giving forces have been made visible in a sculpture. It may happen that a delicate piece of work which at first glance appeared insignificant is found on closer consideration to be especially consistent and carefully executed. It then becomes a kind of "harmonious centre point" by which the pupils can orient their judgement.

A difficult situation arises when one piece is so outstandingly good that many students feel completely overshadowed and lose courage. It is then not easy to do justice to the other exhibits. But the spirit of the class can tolerate the superiority of some. With complete fairness several students, particularly girls, study every exhibit praising the successful ones and gently mocking those that are rather funny because their creator was over-ambitious.

Art lessons most clearly reveal the differences in the students' talents. That is why only certain especially characteristic works are discussed. For, what matters is how the individual expands in his creative work, forgetting everything around him in an effort to express his inner vision. He is then so closely tied up with his creation that he cannot regard it with detachment. Some even shrink from looking at their products together with the rest of the group. But the stronger the community spirit of the class, the sooner they learn to accept criticism.

Since art lessons are given in two-hour block periods, it is possible to achieve a balance between concentrated individual creation and joint appreciation. Sympathetic understanding and fair appraisal based on one's own mastery of the technique employed train an objective critical judgement uninfluenced by subjective taste. A social element also enters into art education. In contrast to technical work, art work has no norms. There is no "recipe" for composition, no fixed rule for colour blending. Personal preferences and distastes for certain colours are legitimate. The experience of such individual differences, which emerge very distinctly in the process of joint appreciation, counterbalances the depersonalization of industrial production the pupils encounter in their technical training. The individualization inherent in every artistic activity should help them to develop into free personalities capable of making creative cultural contributions to the social life of the society.

Ruth Moering

## 2.6.7 *Producing a piece of work for the certificate of apprenticeship*

The crafts and technical training provided by the Hibernia School culminates in the manufacture of an examination piece. This is always an item for practical use. The task includes work-planning, construction and drawings to norm, and calculation and execution, all within a given period of time.

In this work the students apply, independently and on their own responsibility, the knowledge and skills they have acquired in the entire course of their education. The circumspection this calls for cannot be expected of the 17 year olds in Grade 11, but should be within the powers of 18 year olds.

Future electricians usually have to do a complete installation for a house or perhaps the lighting system for the school stage. Mechanical engineers may be asked to make complex tools or devices for the factory in which they have been trained.

The most impressive examination pieces are those of the carpenters. Having practised carving and manufacture of simple boxes and small items of furniture ever since Grade 5, the pupils were familiarized in the second semester of Grade 11 with all aspects of furniture manufacture, from initial discussion with the customer to completion of the article. But they had the teacher to assist them. In Grade 12 they have to work increasingly on their own. The skills they now possess, together with the abilities developed in their theoretical and artistic education, should enable them to solve their tasks imaginatively.

In the latter part of Grade 12 they consider at length what piece of work they should make for their examination. They investigate the construction, specific difficulties and artistic design of all kinds of desk, cupboard, sideboard, etc. to get inspiration and then develop their own suggestions. One student's examination piece is described below as an example.

He had decided to make a desk. A draft drawing, scale 1:10, represented a table standing firmly on the extensions of four vertical boards of the two side drawers. It was an original idea, but it looked too heavy. In the next draft the boards were replaced by eight legs. It still looked rather clumsy. The final draft had the desk resting on four slightly curved legs. But the table top now appeared to have a load-carrying function. Through clever addition of some cross strips the student avoided this impression of heaviness. He had been determined to disregard the basic rule of carpentry, the "golden section"; he had wanted to be guided only by his own aesthetic sense. But when he measured the length/width ratio of the final result of all his trials he found that he had arrived at exactly the proportions of the golden section.

By Christmas he had finished the drafting of design and construction. The technical drawings, working time and price calculations were made in the Christmas holidays, and then he was able to start manufacturing the individual parts of his desk. Exact records of his work were kept, and members of the examination committee (consisting of the teachers concerned and representatives of the Board of Trade, the education authorities and the parents) regularly came to check his progress. He had

135 hours in which to complete the job, but since in his determination to produce a beautiful piece of work he had disregarded the technical difficulties his design entailed, he needed 140 hours. However, this additional time was within the allowed limits.

This student is now in the final general section of the Hibernia School with the intention of entering university.

Josef Meise


2.7   <u>Parents cooperation in an independent school</u>


<u>A parent's report</u>

The year was 1963. Easter was approaching, the date when my eldest son would finish his schooling at a *Volksschule* (elementary plus main school). What was to become of a fourteen year old who at the age of ten had failed to pass the entrance examination to a grammar school? Was his entire life to be ruined by this failure? He had no particular interest in any of the occupations open to him. Besides, none of them would have fostered his intellectual potential or offered him adequate learning opportunities. All my efforts to find a suitable educational institution remained fruitless until I finally heard of the Hibernia School, which at the time was still a full-time vocational and vocational extension school. I was very sceptical because it was a private school, something which I had not previously considered. All I wanted was an establishment where my son could correct the "mistake" he had made at the age of ten. In retrospect I can now understand why so many parents desire to send their children to a state school. They know of too few alternatives.

Soon after my son had been admitted to the Hibernia School. the first parents' meeting took place. We were astonished to find that the class teacher did not talk about achievement goals, marks and school regulations but about the development of man. He told us of the latent talents in every human which must be recognized, activated and promoted. For the first time we heard the names of *Waldorfschule* and *Rudolf Steiner*. We were informed about a special kind of pedagogy, one that is built upon insights into the nature of man. We learnt that there is no repetition of classes at this school, that the boys and girls of each age group stay together until they have completed their schooling.

The curriculum amazed us. We saw that pupils intending to become industrial workers did woodwork, such as rasping planting sticks or making garden furniture. Future fitters, lathe turners, mechanics, electricians or carpenters modelled in clay, painted in watercolour and practised playing the recorder.

Having seen all these unusual school features it should not have surprised us that the class teacher proposed visiting us at home. Nevertheless we were worried. Had our son done something so dreadful that the teacher wished to call on us? We were rather tense as we waited for him. But when he came we only chatted about our son, his siblings and "our" school.

When I had become acquainted with the educational activities at the school, I began to take an interest in its whole background. I started collecting information on Waldorf schools, on Rudolf Steiner and the educational theory he developed. Eventually my wife and I became parent-representatives of the class and thus members of the Parents' Association. Parent-representatives are spokesmen for the parents of a class. They must enjoy the confidence of both the other parents and the class teacher. In each class there are four or five such couples. They do not constitute a "power bloc" within the school, a group acting on its own - parents versus teachers - but work together with the teachers. Their activities include:

1) preparation of the parents' meetings in cooperation with the teacher. They discuss with him the parents' worries and difficulties and he explains his educational intentions to them. In their discussions with the teacher they do not merely ask questions but tell him frankly and critically what they think;

2) preparation of class trips, Christmas bazars, summer festivals and all other school events in cooperation with the class teacher. From my own experience I can now say that all these joint activities are a decisive factor in the life of a school;

3) activation of the other parents - a major task;

4) participation in meetings, held every six weeks, of the "Parents' Association" which includes the parent-representatives of the whole school. In these meetings matters of general concern, such as economic, legal and educational issues and their implications for the school, are discussed from the parents' point of view. To make this circle workable, a group of six to ten parents are elected to form the Parent's Advisory Council. This Council prepares the meetings of the Parents' Association and clarifies problems arising in them in subsequent individual conversations with the teachers.

In 1964 the school moved into the new buildings. Although the first building stage had landed it with a debt of DM 5 million, we were happy to have, at last, rooms and a building of our own.

New legislation, the changed economic situation in industry and, last not least, the increasingly intricate and time-consuming accounting procedure prescribed by the educational authorities made the "Enterprise Hibernia School" - probably the biggest citizens' initiative in the educational sector of North-Rhine-Westphalia - an economic tightrope act.

It should be mentioned that it is also "parents' cooperation" when the parents at our school provide DM 800,000 year after year in order to close the gap in the school budget between actual expenditure and the grant from the province North-Rhine-Westphalia, which does not take into account the fact that an independent school uses neither local nor state buildings or equipment.

When the development of the school had reached the point where the functions of the Head were largely taken over by a collegiate body, the members of the School Association Board assumed full responsibility for the economic and legal position of the school. Three parents and three teachers trained themselves for this task and now administer an annual budget of DM 5 million and buildings valued at some DM 12 million.

One major item in parents' cooperation is the reception and involvement of new parents. Ever since our school was established, teachers have had educational talks with all new children and their parents. Up to 1972 the discussions with

new parents about their financial contributions to the school
and their share in its assets were conducted by the managers
of the school administration or their deputies. Later, awareness of the parents' co-responsibility led a group of parents
to take on this job. A Parents' Contribution Committee was
formed, and now these matters are arranged entirely among parents. It is no easy task, considering that six to eight parents
have to conduct some one hundred individual discussions with
newcomers per year.

All of us, teachers as well as parents, have adopted the
principle that the necessity of part-financing by the parents
should not turn our school into an institution for well-to-do
people. We are determined that it should truly reflect the
social structure of its environment, an industrial area. This
implies that more affluent parents should make bigger financial
contributions than the others. In these talks about contributions and the resulting agreements the parents bear responsibility and take decisions on behalf of the school.

Another important component of parents' cooperation is
the presence of representatives at the final examinations for
officially recognized certificates, a duty which may take a
whole week out of our holiday. Two factors motivated the parents to accept this commitment: first, we want to demonstrate
that everything that happens at the school, in particular the
examinations, is also the parents' concern. Second, our presence encourages the examinees.

The above list of parents' cooperation tasks is neither
inflexible nor final. If and when questions or problems arise
in the school's everyday life - be it from outside or within
the school community - *ad hoc* initiative groups are formed;
when the matter concerned is cleared up they dissolve. It may
also be mentioned that in addition to cooperation at our school,
parents-representatives contact with the other Waldorf schools.
They attend parents' or parent-teacher meetings there, exchange
experiences and communicate new ideas. Lectures and weekend
meetings at our own or in neighbourhood schools round off the
picture.

Parents who have experienced such communal activities
cannot, and should not, cut themselves off from the school when
their children have completed their education. As members of
the League of Friends ex-parents and ex-pupils continue to take
part in its life. I shall certainly do so when younger parents

have taken over my present commitments.

> Werner Harder
> Parents' delegate in the
> School Association Committee

## 2.8 Financing, legal status and organization of the Hibernia School. Collegiate management and self-administration

The Hibernia School has some 1000 pupils, 74 teaching personnel, 10 staff members in the administrative and service sectors, a creche and kindergartens, a hostel, productively operating workshops and various social amenities. In 1976 its budget was DM 5 million. Of this, DM 3.780,000 were personnel costs, DM 520,000 administrative material costs and DM 150,000 building investments. The remainder was spent on miscellaneous items, such as school meals, interest on loans, special teacher training, school library, etc.

### 2.8.1 *Financial position*

As the School has to finance its own buildings, efforts are made to keep the building costs as low as possible. The final cost of the first set of buildings amounted to DM 94 per cubic metre as against the normal estimate of DM 120 for primary schools and DM 160 for grammar schools. As a result of the time-tabling for Grades 11 and 12, a 40 hour per week utilization of many classrooms and workshops is achieved, while the estimated average for state schools comes to 32 hours per week. Additionally, school room is saved by the fact that Hibernia School pupils take their leaving certificates in a shorter time than is usual. Altogether the expenditure on buildings and equipment is thus some 30 - 40% lower than that of state schools plus industrial training establishments providing the same level of education.

Despite the fact that the Hibernia School curriculum includes many art courses not given at other schools, the overall cost of 12 years' education up to the advanced technical school certificate plus the certificate of apprenticeship is lower than that of 10 years' education in a state school plus three years of apprenticeship in an industrial training workshop. The same applies to the dual qualification for university entrance plus certificate of apprenticeship. Although certification is not the real educational goal of the Hibernia School, it achieves this in 14 years, whereas it takes 15 years to obtain the same qualifications elsewhere (13 years' schooling plus 2 - 3 years of apprenticeship).

With the exception of five additional teachers engaged in administrative and development work that is done for other schools by outside institutions, the Hibernia School's teaching staff is of the same size as that of state schools. However, it carries a heavier work load. The teachers have to spend a considerable amount of time and energy on visits to parents, preparation of festivals and dramatic performances and on conferences. Moreover, many disturbed or handicapped children are cured at the School, so that it also fulfils to a certain extent the functions of a special school or renders attendance at a special school unnecessary by arresting the development of incipient handicaps.

The teachers' salaries are subsidized by the state to the tune of 94% of equivalent state school teachers' salaries. The remaining 6% must be covered out of the School's own resources. The same applies to the costs of power, maintenance, and materials.

Of the school's total expenditure of DM 5 million, DM 1 million is not covered by state grants. This 20% is raised by

1) parents' contributions (see 2.7). In 1975 the parents contributed a total of DM 754,000 i.e. DM 67 per month and per child;

2) staff members' contributions of part of their salaries;

3) voluntary contributions by private individuals or institutions (mostly members of the League of Friends of the Hibernia School).

The large sum that must be raised by the parents presents a serious problem. Despite all efforts to adjust the contributions to the individual parents' circumstances, they are too high for the less well-paid families (industrial workers, craftsmen or office employees) of roughly 50% of the Hibernia School pupils.

## 2.8.2 Legal status of the Hibernia School as an independent school

Like other independent schools, the Hibernia School is subject to the *Ersatzschule* (alternative school) legislation. It is approved as a comprehensive school of its own kind and has the status of an "Alternative School" equivalent to first-level school, *Hauptschule*, full time vocational school and advanced technical school, as well as to the technical school for social work and institutions leading to university entrance. In other words, its pupils obtain the same qualifications they would acquire at these other schools.

Its teaching personnel must have a licence to teach from the educational authorities. This is usually granted on the basis of an education equivalent to that of teachers at state school. Some exceptions are, however, possible under the relevant legislation of North-Rhine-Westphalia.

The body legally responsible for the Hibernia School is the "Hibernia School Association". Its members are parents and teachers. Both have equal representation on the Association Board, which makes legally valid appointments and dismissals on behalf of the various school conferences and committees.

It is also responsible for the financial operations of the school within the meaning of German association law.

Individuals and institutions willing to support the school materially or in non-material ways are combined in the "League of Friends of the Hibernia School". The "Hibernia School Foundation" consists of parents, teachers and prominent persons in public life. It owns the social grounds, buildings and equipment, which have largely been financed by loans that must now be gradually repaid out of parents' contributions. The Foundation also manages facilities that form part of the school system but do not constitute "school" in the narrower sense of the word, such as school workshops, school kitchen, hostel for pupils, teachers' housing.

## 2.8.3 *Internal organization*

### a) Management

*The Internal Conference*

The collegiate body responsible for the school management is called the Internal Conference. It meets regularly once a week. At present it has 50 members, teaching personnel as well as other staff. It is responsible for the execution of the decisions of the Hibernia School Association and for the overall direction of the school. Its working procedures may be described as follows:

1) Discussion of matters concerning the school as a whole, such as definition of its educational goals, its role in a differentiated national education system, the implications of economic and political changes, the plans of new staff members, curricular changes, etc.

2) Establishment of committees to deal with the operational aspects of the outcomes of these discussions. Non-members of the Internal Conference may also become committee members.

3) Receiving the committes' reports on problems they consider particularly important. This practice creates in the Conference members a differentiated problem awareness, while providing the committee members with comments, a check and correction of their work.

4) Ensuring personnel rotation in the membership of the committees; setting up new committees to investigate new issues arising from the School's overall strategy; and terminating existing committees when they have completed their tasks.

5) Interviewing applicants for teaching posts who have been shortlisted by the Personnel Committee and specialist commities, and sanctioning or amending the proposed decisions.

*Committees*

1) School Management Committee. - Contact and correspondence with parents, authorities, inquirers; outside representation of the school; drafting

and supervising of organizational arrangements, such as supervision during breaks, class trips, school events such as monthly festivals, theatre performances, holiday periods; checking on punctual commencement of lessons; organization and running of examinations; representation of the school within the Union of Waldorf schools; direction of the "Technical Conference" (see b) 4)); awareness of latent, as yet unidentified tasks and their further treatment.

To enable this committee to obtain an overall view of what happens at the school and what problems exist, it must include members of the Time-tabling, Personnel and Events Committees as well as members of the Internal and the Educational Conference.

Acute or short-term problems are dealt with by three members of the School Management Committee. They must be available for talks with colleagues at definite times every day.

2) Time-tabling Committee. - Identification, in cooperation with the specialist groups, of lesson time requirements of the individual subjects; establishment of lesson and block period time-tables on the basis of these requirements; supervision of this organizational pattern, amendments; substitutions.

3) Personnel Committee. - Planning of personnel requirements in cooperation with the Time-tabling Committee; recruitment of applicants, sifting of applications and relevant correspondence with the authorities in cooperation with the specialist groups and the Internal Conference; salary and retirement matters.

4) Steering Committe for the Internal Conference. - Pre-analysis of problems; agendas; chairing of discussions.

5) Steering Committee for the Lower School Conference. (Grades 1-8). - Pre-analysis of educational organization problems; agendas; chairing of discussions.

6) Steering Committee for the Upper School Conference (Grades 9-14). - Breakdown of educa-

tional organization problems; agendas; chairing of discussions.

7) Admissions Committee. - Admission of new pupils (excluding arrangement of parents' financial contributions) in cooperation with class teachers; control of class composition in accordance with established criteria (e.g. social aspects, differing abilities, geographical area).

8) Mediation Committee. - Mediation in cases of differences of opinions or conflicts.

9) Budget Committee. - Administration of budget for teaching aids (excluding books); duty travel, journeys to conferences.

10) Events Committee. - Planning, technical/financial responsibility for and running of school events, performances by outside artists (concerts, recitations, eurhythmy, etc.), lectures, conferences within the school; establishment of an annual programme for these events and programming of pupils' performances, such as dramatic performances by individual grades, concerts, monthly festivals.

11) Library- and Text-book Committee. - Ascertaining of requirements and ordering of text-books; organization of library (integration of provision for teachers and for pupils); enlargement of library; administration of library budget; encouraging teachers and pupils to use the library as a working tool.

12) Building Committee. - Maintenance control of school buildings and equipment.

13) Parents Contribution Committee. - Financial discussions with newcomers and agreements on contributions.

In addition, there are committees for temporary tasks, such as educational projects, the summer festival, the Christmas bazaar.

Once established, the committees have considerable operational freedom within the area of their mandate. They are, however, responsible to the Internal Conference. There should be a kind of flowing balance: on the one hand the committees must not minimize their obligation to report to the Internal Conference, on the other hand the Conference must not interfere with the committees' operational independence. An omnipotent Internal Conference which did not delegate decisions would be so overloaded with work that it would be unable to function properly; entirely self-responsible committees might isolate themselves to such an extent that their decisions might conflict with the other aspects of the school. The committees' competence develops in the course of working on their special tasks. The experiences, insights and factual understanding they gain in this work from the basis for competent decision. This is the same principle by which the teachers are given responsibility for organizing their lessons.

Membership of the committees rotates, but is never changed all at once. After serving for a while on one committee every teacher thus has a chance of participating in others and acquiring decision competence in different fields. This rhythmic change of learning situations and learning settings may be considered a special form of lifelong learning. It also develops the teachers' personalities. Social abilities can only be acquired through practice, including verification, correction and self-experience. Nobody may, therefore, be dismissed from a committee until his term of membership has expired. Every member should be permitted to work in an atmosphere of confidence, support and toleration of beginner's mistakes, for which he must, however, accept responsibility.

Such experiences are valuable lessons not only for the individual but also for the whole school community, which continuously learns from its system of self-administration. The task areas entrusted to the committees, the way in which they carry out their jobs and cooperate with other committees, are constantly changed as new insights are achieved. The above description of collegiate administration, as well as that of conference work below, is therefore to be regarded not as a rigid system but as a snapshot of the present stage in a development determined both by changing external conditions and by growing insights and differing abilities. (5)

b) <u>Professional meetings ("Conferences")</u>

In addition to the Internal Conference, there are a number of regular staff meetings called "Conferences":

1) The General Educational Conference. - All members of the educational staff take part in this conference, in which

   - the fundamental theoretical work of the teaching staff is done;
   - selected classes or pupils are discussed;
   - examples of curriculum content and methods (selected block periods, teaching projects, etc.) are presented.

   The General Educational Conference provides part of the institutionalized continued education for the teaching staff.

2) Lower and Upper School Conferences. - In these conferences

   - classes and pupils are discussed; where necessary, special educational measures are developed;
   - educational projects and new plans are analyzed and followed through;
   - problems concerning several or all lower or upper grades are identified.

3) Class Conferences. - These conferences are convened by the class teacher or class counsellor or by the Lower or Upper School Conferences. They deal with

   - marking and admission to examinations;
   - detailed examination of the educational and psychological conditions of individual pupils, groups of pupils or the whole class;
   - promotion of pupils to the upper grades.

   The individual specialist groups (metalwork, woodwork, art, English, mathematics, social studies, etc.) work out, in cooperation with the Internal Conference and the Time-tabling Committee, the handling and further development of their respective curricula, including methodological and didactic issues of lesson organization, such as regular or block period lessons, size of groups, distribution of teachers.

4) The Technical Conference. - This conference
   - deals with organizational and technical information and problems concerning the whole school, such as holiday dates, school regulations and supervision, personal matters;
   - discusses the programme of special events presented by the Events Committee.

The major conferences are held every Thursday afternoon:

15.45 - 17.15 General Educational Conference
17.30 - 18.30 Lower and Upper School Conferences
18.45 - 19.30 Technical Conference
19.30 - 20.00 Dinner
20.00 - 22.30 Internal Conference.

Class Conferences, Examination Conferences, and Specialist Conferences are arranged as need arises.

c) The development of self-administration

Waldorf pedagogy, striving for a live, all-round education, presupposes that each staff member feels responsible for the whole, self-determining school. Experience has shown that, when a teaching staff develops from small beginnings, the capacities of its individual members grow with it. Though there comes a time when administrative tasks have to be divided up, the feeling of overall responsibility remains and fosters cooperation. This feeling originates in the last analysis from ever expanding insights in the fields of educational theory and the study of man, and from the experience that these insights hold good in practice.

The form of organization that has been described has developed in the course of some seven years. In general it may be said that a type of communication which makes it possible to take joint decisions can only be achieved in a climate of personal alertness and frankness among colleagues. Rigid routine forms of administration do not tolerate individual initiative, and a bureaucratic, conventional attitude - "It's always been done like that" - obstructs innovation.

On the other hand, good will alone is useless and may even be detrimental, in the absence of factual understanding. Committee members must thoroughly familiarize themselves with the overall context of their tasks; they must acquire new knowledge enabling them to foresee the implications of their decisions for the school as a whole. The danger that a certain degree of inflexible expertise may develop in the course of time is averted by the rotation principle governing all committees. Constant reviews of the existing organization ensure its continuous further development. Individual learning in the social domain and a constantly developing form of organization thus condition one another. Although a risk of stagnation is always there, it can be overcome by the individuals' active engagement, by their live interest in each other, by tolerance and "confidence in the spirit dwelling in the other". The better the staff succeed in creating this climate among themselves, the more will it spread to the relations between teachers and older pupils and between teachers and parents - provided that it remains possible for all to know each other and to contact each other at any time. Certainly, this requires an effort not needed in schools that are administered from outside. But it awakens creative social forces, namely the ability to keep a balance between free initiative and critical reflection. These forces are constantly needed in human relationships but are often lacking; even at the Hibernia School they are not yet fully developed. In this respect self-administering independent schools could become a model for new forms of life in our society.

NOTES

(1) An example is given in Appendix 1.

(2) Rudolf Steiner started developing the eurhythmic art of movement (visible language and visible song) in 1912. It is part of the curriculum in all Waldorf schools.

(3) In 1969-71 two parallel Grade 11 and Grade 12 classes were dissolved and reorganized, each into three smaller groups of roughly equal ability level. It was found that the weaker pupils had had much stronger learning motivation in the old class community. After two years of experimentation the previous pattern of class community lasting to the end of Grade 12 was, therefore, restored.

(4) This combination of artistic creation and educational guidance has been developed in cooperation with the *Werklehrer- und Bildhauerschule* of the *Goetheanum* in Dornach/ Switzerland.

(5) In the development of this form of organization aiming at lifelong learning by the individual and at a learning process involving the entire system, the Hibernia School has been assisted by the "Nederlands Paedagogisch Institut voor het Bedrijfslernen" at Zeist/ Netherlands.

CHAPTER 3


EDUCATIONAL ASPECTS OF RUDOLF STEINER'S "STUDY OF MAN"
AND THEIR APPLICATION IN THE HIBERNIA SCHOOL

The basis of the educational conception of Rudolf Steiner schools is Steiner's anthroposophical *Study of Man*. Interested readers are referred to the section on Rudolf Steiner's writings and lectures in the attached bibliography. Those of his insights that are especially significant for an understanding of what he calls "the art of education", which all Waldorf educational institutions, including kindergartens and therapeutic establishments, attempt to realize, are described in this chapter with special reference to the particular concepts and methodological principles developed from them by the Hibernia School.

## 3.1 Development phases and the changing nature of learning

Most immediately significant for Steiner's art of education is that human development throughout childhood and adolescence occurs in phases. It is stimulated by learning processes and at the same time determines the particular manner in which learning takes place in these successive phases.

These development phases may encompass relatively short or long periods of time marked by physical and psychological changes. The two most important dividing lines, recognized very early by Steiner and corroborated by decades of experience, are the change of teeth (at approximately 7 years of age) and puberty (approximately 14 years of age). The special character of each of the three phases may be illustrated by the way in which the child learns from the educator.

In the first phase (age 1 - 7) it is stimulated directly by what the educator does and how he does it, by what he feels, says and thinks. The child imitates both his gestures and his inner attitude; it assimilates a differentiated or an impoverished language, richness or poverty of feeling and thinking.

In the second phase (age 8 - 14), the main contact beteween teacher and learner lies in the psychological sphere of sensation and feeling. The child seeks in the educator a revered or admired authority. A stable and differentiated communication is now needed to educate the child. The more its feelings (admiration or repulsion, tension or satisfaction, etc.) are involved, the better it will learn.

In the third phase (age 15 - 21) the learner wants to see reasons, to understand. The relationship between teacher and learner thus lies on the plane of reflective consciousness and independent judgement. The learner should be increasingly permitted to choose whom he will personally accept as his teacher.

These three principal phases comprise many intermediate and transitional stages, and the teacher is faced with a variety of individual modifications of this general development process. He must recognize whether precocious or retarded entry into a particular stage indicates a special developmental type or whether it is due to external or internal peculiarities. In every case he sees his task in stabilizing individual expansion. An important means of doing so is to incorporate these widely varying development processes into one comprehensive group process. If the teacher succeeds in building up an educationally effective grouping by means of appropriate educational measures, such groups achieve their own developmental rhythm. They are capable of carrying retarded developments and protecting advanced ones.

An education oriented by the child's individual development phases and resulting learning needs can only be organized in the form of a school if the individual development processes are so incorporated in a group process. And this is only justified when processes of mutual assistance, promotion and complementation take place within the group, for instance in a class of children of equal age. Steiner's works, in particular his views of human temperaments and how they can be utilized in group processes, will be of considerable help to the educator.

## 3.2 Differentiation in the process of becoming a complete human being, need for comprehensiveness and specifity of learning provision

Another insight of great importance concerns the inner differentiations occurring in the process of becoming a complete human being, and the recognition that these processes will only lead to full expansion of the individual's personality if they are stimulated and facilitated by appropriate learning provision.

Human individuality has its roots in the fields of tension of numerous inner polarities. The most important of these are the polarities of insight and action, of individual and social identification, of conservation and change. These fields of tension resulting from spiritual differentiation must also be built up in the course of the development processes in childhood and youth. Whether or not this differentiation is initiated and facilitated depends on the specificity and comprehensiveness of the learning provision. Any learning provision is specific, because it necessarily involves a selection. Its specificity is educationally justified when, as has already been mentioned, it corresponds to the particular learning disposition of the development phase concerned, and when it is especially suited to facilitate the developmental step from which this learning disposition results. However, these learning dispositions spread out in various directions in the course of this spiritual differentiation process. The degree to which the whole range of differentiating potential is developed depends on the comprehensiveness of the learning provision. The conception of the Hibernia School, in particular the consistent structuring of a programme of practical learning, attempts to fulfil this task. In the following, an outline will be sketched of the views and basic methodological patterns offered by the anthroposophical study of man on which this concept is based.

### 3.2.1 *The interrelationship of theory and practice and the pedagogical significance of art*

In the first few years of life, experience consciousness is still inseparably bound up with physical activity. That is why at this stage of development the child learns exclusively through its senses, by imitation. What it experiences in its environment it imitates directly with its body. Inversely, it can only experience as much of the world as it can actively seize or taste, touch, move or run around. Its feelings become conscious only when they manifest themselves physically.

If we contrast this with the psychological configuration of an adult, the change in the child's development process that is necessary for it to arrive at differentiation becomes immediately clear. In adults the processes of consciousness have been internalized, largely separated from the processes of physical activity. The highest stage of consiousness as represented, for instance, by purely conceptual thought, is independent of any external physical action.

This gradual extrication of thinking consciousness from its original entanglement with physical processes occurs in the course of cognitive education. An educational anthropology must try to discover the stages through which this extrication passes, the forms of consciousness (image, idea, concept) in which the respective advances in development manifest themselves, and the way in which these correlate with the child's overall development.

The *Study of Man* shows that the will operative in thinking consciousness corresponds with the life processes of the body and its outward activity. "Man thinks by the same forces by which he grows and lives. But these forces must die so that he will become a thinker." (1) This insight explains a transfer effect which has been observed and must be taken into account in conceiving a course of cognitive education, namely that purposeful training in the motor domain has repercussions on cognitive learning development. It is not sufficient to foster the development of consciousness by offering appropriate, that is to say age-related, contents. Rather must the will which is operative in physical processes first be directed onto a higher developmental level before the corresponding step in cognitive development can be taken. Every new step in the acquisition of skill, reaction, concentration on work manifests not merely a purposeful motor development but is at the same time a foundation for a development of consciousness (see, for instance, 2.3.2 and 2.3.7).

However, the objective must not merely be to guide the child towards reflective consciousness of its actions. It must also learn to direct its actions by this reflective consciousness. Only he who *acts* from such consciousness attains freedom. It is here that art assumes its important function in education. For both in artistic awareness and in personal artistic production the capacity actively to combine reflection and action is practised. In the first school years all learning processes are, therefore, interlinked with artistic designing (see 2.3.3). At the higher level a third learning area of a distinctive nature, methodically directed artistic practice, is interspersed between academic learning and practical learning. Its purpose is to enable the young to integrate theory and practice in an active and artistic manner both in their consciousness and in their actions.

3.2.2 *Differentiation in individual and social learning*

The adult feels confronted with a dual challenge. He must continually re-identify with himself (individuation) and he must also continually identify with his social environment (socialization). From this dialectic tension results the experience of individuality. He must, therefore, have developed this dual nature in the process of his education and must have learnt to bring the two areas to fruitful interaction. Through his ability to build up his own fields of interest he can expand his individual self; through his ability to perceive the needs and requirements of his social environment and to change them by discerning action, his individual self gains an identity.

Here again the educator who conceives of his educational task as enabling the growing child to realize its all-round and differentiated potential through learning, is faced with the problem as to how he can guide it in such a manner that this differentiation takes a healthy form. The crucial point is to provide comprehensive learning stimulation at all stages so as to facilitate all-round development. *Individual learning is based on cognitive development and social learning on motor development*. This explains why hardly any social learning occurs in the present general school system, which provides virtually no practical learning.

But individual and social competence must not be developed separately. These two poles of personality expansion must also be brought into fruitful interaction. This is facilitated by group learning. Just as the individual capacity to integrate theory and practice grows out of an artistic approach to all learning processes, so learning in a pedagogically designed grouping is the crucial means of realizing the inter-conditioning of individual and social learning. The child experiences how its individual expansion is fostered by mutual assistance within its group, and how its knowledge and skills do not attain significance until they become effective in a common learning process. Group pedagogy is, therefore, a core element of an education adapted to the specific requirements of each developmental and learning stage.

### 3.2.3 *Memory, imagination and creativity*

In addition to the relationship between theory and practice and between individual and social learning, there is a third field of tension in man. It is the polarity of conservation and change, the living interaction of which is of fundamental importance for the attainment of independent individuality. The archetype of this situation is the process of individual development into a complete human being. In this process the essence of the child's personality first changes its physical condition to match the core of its nature. This is possible only if it constructs an entirely new body within the broad pattern of the original, inherited body. This process takes place in the early years of life and manifests itself in phenomena such as change of teeth and the so-called children's diseases.

Other given factors moulding the learning child are the way of life, the forms of expression and the conventions of its social environment. The child must acquire these in such a manner that it has them at its command without allowing them to govern its personality. In other words, it must be capable of accepting, performing, applying them as well as of changing them and progressing through change. One of these two poles in the psyche, the ability to conserve, finds its expression in memory, the other, the power to change, in imagination. Both forces must be understood as interconnected, as a polarity, if they are to be effectively developed in the child. This means that either characteristic can only be developed in the direction of human expansion if it is aroused and stimulated in interrelation with the other. The same applies to the training of memory and imagination. Memory is the power to collect and conserve in consciousness (knowledge), imagination the power to change and produce anew (design). Bare knowledge is in danger of rigidifying. It must be acquired in a manner which will give it an instrumental character, make it material for man's own inner productivity. Similarly, mere wealth of imagination has no value. It must connect with given conditions, with the external situation and with inner experiences, if change is to constitute progress.

The art of education as practised in Rudolf Steiner schools is governed by this postulate. It aims to induce the learner to build up and assimilate knowledge with the aid of his imagination, and to combine the acquisition of skills with reflection and insight.

In the early school years, when the child's psychological capacities are still largely undifferentiated, these two processes are closely interlaced in the lessons. Thereafter the learning provision branches out into matter requiring progressively more reflective (academic) and more active (practical) learning processes, and interrelation between the two becomes a clearly recognizable method in the teaching of both areas. It is a vital precondition for inner expansion and independence (emancipation) of the personality that memory and imagination develop in a process of mutual stimulation. Out of the gradual intensification of this polarity grows a third power, one that is increasingly being recognized as the principal foundation for man's inner and outward independence: creativity. It can only be initiated and individually developed in a process that is itself creative. That is why education, the initiation and implementation of learning processes, must be practised as an art, and why the whole spectrum of artistic means - painting/modelling, speaking/dramatics and music - is so indispensable for appropriate learning processes.

## 3.3  Growth to full humanity as self-realization

### 3.3.1 *The cultural development of humanity and the role of learning*

In his educational study Rudolf Steiner has arrived at a third fundamental insight. Human development is characterized not only by proceeding in phases, each of which has a distinct quality of its own, and by progressive differentiation and polarization of the personality, but also by the fact that the course of this development is not an inevitable process ordained by nature. It occurs only when it is willed by man himself; it is a process of self-realization.

In earlier stages of man's historical progress towards full humanity this self-realization was a group process; the individual did not choose it by himself. In the contemporary stage of the process, self-realization can only be achieved by self-directed development. The autonomy of consciousness that is possible today must lead to an autonomy of individual development.

The instrument by which a new impulse can be given at every stage of the development towards full humanity is learning. What has been said about human development applies equally to learning: it occurs only when it is consciously initiated and facilitated, when it is willed. Recent research results show that the naturally given dispositions, that is the genetic potential, such as speech or thought, do not come to full fruition, if the necessary learning impulses are missing or inadequate, as they may be, for instance, in a specific social environment. The questions then arise under what conditions learning facilitates human development in a child, and how the learning process must be designed so that it will lead from guided to self-directed learning.

3.3.2 *Necessity of development-specific learning provision. The issue of age-relatedness*

The age-relatedness of learning provision in the Hibernia School has been repeatedly stressed in the preceding chapters. Its central significance for the pedagogy of this School and of all other educational institutions guided by Rudolf Steiner's philosophy should, therefore, be evident to the reader. When it has been recognized that human development occurs in phases and depends at each phase on the learning opportunities provided, it will be asked what specific problems and intentions, what special forms of consciousness and behaviour, correspond to each of these stages, and what specific learning provision is capable of initiating the particular step on the road to becoming a complete human being which is appropriate and possible at each stage. How the Hibernia School tries to answer these questions is described in detail in paragraphs 3.4 ff.

3.3.3 *Education for freedom. From guided to self-directed learning*

To initiate individual learning competence in his pupils, the teacher must himself be competent. For it is not only the learning contents, selected according to the learner's age, which stimulate the humane development of a child, but also the personality of the teacher who mediates these contents.

His own development as a learner motivates the child. Hence an educator can help to develop in a child only those qualities that he himself possesses or of which he has had personal experience.

This fact has implications. An art of education aiming to guide the child towards self-directed learning, to facilitate the acquisition of competence, must be based on the educator's free decision. He must know the laws governing child development, and he must know that they are not laws of nature but become effective only when they are accepted and consciously realized. Through meditative practice he must have them so present in his mind that he can recognize the special character of individual development and respond to it by designing his teaching accordingly.

To organize learning adapted to individual development in the form of a school, its contents, volume and timing must be planned. The curriculum should describe the learning processes that are to be facilitated and state which particular development is to be initiated, continued or stabilized by the learning process concerned. The reasons for the selection of subject matter from the point of view of learning development should also be given. To that extent the contents specified in the curriculum are only of an illustrative nature; it is quite possible that in a particular case some other subject matter may be much more effective in achieving the desired development. Hence the curriculum serves merely as a framework for the teacher permitting him to solve creatively the problems arising in concrete educational situations. In creative handling of group processes, in building up educationally effective groups he produces his own instruments for uniting the diverse individual learning developments of his class towards a comprehensive joint development.

Such educational action responding directly to the developmental needs of the children demands an "organization of freedom". The inner autonomy of the teacher that is necessary for the phased development of children must have its counterpart in outer independence. Hence the common aims and mutual promotion of those striving together within the school to further the children's learning development call for a collegiate structure, for regular communication (see 2.8).

Only under such conditions can learning be so organized that it will be entirely directed by the goal of guiding the young to the point where they will be able to fulfil themselves in accordance with their individuality in a process of lifelong learning. The fundamental conviction of a self-responsible educator that all his decisions must be taken "on behalf" of the child creates a situation in which he himself is a permanent learner. This learning while teaching corresponds directly to the inner growth of the child and calls forth the creative power latent in his personality, which is the basic element of true learning competence. For self-directed learning is a creative process. It is the realization of freedom.

## 3.4 Principles deriving from the special approach of the Hibernia School

### 3.4.1 *Art and craft work as preliminary stages of a technical education*

In the summer of 1919, immediately before the first school founded and directed by Rudolf Steiner was opened, he wrote in an essay on "The pedagogical foundations of Waldorf Schools":

> "The way in which modern industry has infiltrated the development of human societal life patterns the practice of the new social movement. Parents who are going to entrust their children to this school will needs expect that these children will be educated and taught so as to acquire living competence which takes full account of this movement. It follows that from the very beginning this school must be guided by educational principles rooted in the requirements of contemporary life. The children should be so educated that they become full human beings and are capable of meeting those requirements which any man can espouse, regardless of the conventional social class from which he comes. What the practice of contemporary life demands of men must be reflected in the facilities offered by this school. The spirit active in and dominating that life must be stimulated in the children through education and instruction." (2)

At approximately the same time Steiner talked in his lectures on national education about the characteristics of a "technical culture", preparation for which he considered to be the vital task of the general educational system.

The special approach of the Hibernia School is to develop an educational conception through which the young will be comprehensively prepared for participation in a technical culture.

In a previously unimaginable way industrial technology and the living conditions resulting from it have weakened man's ties with society and nature. At the same time the technocratically determined relationships - and this applies particularly to the world of work - have enmeshed him in a system of situational constraints, to such an extent that not only his independence, but his essential humanity are menaced. This happened because the full challenge of the new order had not been foreseen; even now the young are not being prepared for it. No individual will be able to retain his independence in our contemporary working world unless an emancipatory education has endowed him with the practical capacity to do so. An education is emancipatory only when it enables the young to expand and stabilize their individual personlities before they confront the conditions prevailing in a civilization dominated by technology. The aim is not adaptation to society, knowledge and technology but the ability to participate in these areas responsibly and creatively. This aim cannot be reached unless education is oriented by the laws of human development and sees the technical and social changes of our time as a stage in this development.

3.4.2 *Practical skill, usefulness and necessity are basic elements of technical education*

The special nature of preparation for responsible participation in a technical civilization emerges most clearly in the preparation for working life. What are the modes and objectives of an education which aims to enable a young person to take his place in the highly specialized employment system of an industrialized society with its division of labour, and to humanize it?

Human activity becomes economically and socially meaningful work when it satisfies human needs. To produce such work the young must learn three things:
1) they must acquire enough practical skill in handling materials and tools to enable them to achieve their purpose;

2) they must learn to plan their work functionally so that the result will be usable;

3) they must learn to apprehend the needs of others so thoroughly that the result of their work will meet these needs by being not only usable but necessary.

It is these three factors that turn human activity into work. The same applies to the stage of technical production, in which they assume still wider significance. The manufacture of machines and apparatus, the establishing of organization and procedures, require considerable practical skill, even though this skill is then absorbed by these machines and procedures and becomes independent. Whoever works in that planned technical world must in principle be capable of producing its machinery himself, and he must be able critically to understand its rationality. Only then can he use it as an instrument and change it. Otherwise he will be dependent on it, become its "handyman". Comprehensive practical skill and understanding that will increase as new specialities of technical work are mastered must, however, be developed before entry into the world of industrial work, which cannot itself generate or expand them.

In regard to the postulate of usability the position is similar. The contemporary industrial working world is more functional and planned than it has ever been before. As a result, work processes are so fragmented that their overall purpose can no longer be experienced in individual jobs. The worker must, therefore, have learnt to act out of his previously acquired capacity for insight. He must feel an elementary need to justify his work to himself. So prepared he will be motivated to participate actively in achieving the overall purposes even where the significance of his specific job to the whole process is not immediately evident.

The most important change in human work brought about by industrialization is a social one. It is the fact that nobody can live directly on what he produces; his work serves entirely to meet the needs of others. (3) However, this "objective altruism" only becomes a free action, and as such an expression of social responsibility, when the worker has learnt to see the social usefulness of his work, when he recognizes its necessity. This demands changes in the social form of the contemporary work system. It also requires a kind of education by which such social awareness is prepared and facilitated at all stages of the child's development.

The recognition that the wide opportunities offered by a technical culture can only be utilized by man if he has passed through preliminary stages of a non-technical kind in the course of his education has increasingly become the major determinant of the conception of the Hibernia School. In particular, it has led to a practical course of education extending from play to work for others. If a youth is to put the same commitment into his work as he did into his play as a child, the desire to be able to achieve something, to do something for others, must have already been aroused in the young child. Expanded step by step as he grows older and thus internalized, this desire can become a force guiding his entire life. As has been described in Chapter 2, the early practical tasks given to the child are determined by his own and his parents' personal needs which he will easily understand (see 2.3.2, 2.3.4, 2.3.6 and 2.3.9).

At the stage of crafts activities the pupils still work on orders received from their close environment, but increasingly from people they did not know before, whom they only get to know through those orders and whose requirements they have to discover (2.3.10, 2.6.3). Thus the working targets of the learner become more and more depersonalized until they reach the distance peculiar to technical production. This distance implies an alienation from the work product which calls for a new power of social commitment acquired in this graduated course of practical education.

Work competence also includes the ability to solve a given task independently (see 2.3.12). Again this power, in which planning, execution and evaluation are carried out by different persons, must be developed before entry into the world of technical production. But nobody will be able to plan in a socially justified manner unless he can himself execute what he has thought out. And nobody should have to execute what he could not, in principle, have planned or invented himself, what is beyond mental grasp. That is why from the very start of the practical course given by the Hibernia School all tasks are so selected that the solutions can be jointly developed (2.4.13). The learner tries out his own designs and executes them independently, but under the cooperative responsibility of the workshop instructor.

A similar technique is employed to develop a capacity for self-evaluation and cooperation. Technical work is work ordered by thought. Its results can no longer be checked by personal use but must be evaluated by thought. This is done with the

aid of norms and clearly defined procedures. To reach that
stage the adolescents must have learnt in the course of their
development to work to measurements (2.4.7). In the early
stages the measurements should impose themselves directly from
the function of the product. They should be affectively grasped
by the child and have the nature of aesthetic judgement (see
2.3.3, 2.3.6).

The experience of being able to determine their own
measurements and to evaluate themselves in the manufacturing
process is of great importance at the stage of puberty. But
the object produced must still be immediately meaningful, as
it is in craft work (see 2.4.9). Those who have learnt to work
to exact, self-set measurements, who have experienced how a
work process can be divided up among a working team (2.2.13),
will remain independent when specifications are given to them
by others, as is the rule in technical production. And even
where the division of labour has been planned by the management, they will be aware of being part of a team working towards a common end.

All the foregoing explanations serve to clarify why art
and craft work at the Hibernia School is seen as the preliminary stage of a technical education, and why it is considered
indispensable if the pupils are to be enabled to participate
with social competence in the work processes of a technical
culture. Chapter 2 of this book has described how these intentions are put into practice in the conception and constant
further development of the practical course of education at the
Hibernia School. The following section will outline how age-relatedness finds expression in the curriculum.


3.4.3 *Age-relatedness in the practical components of education*

At the time children usually enter school they are involved in a major inner transformation. Forces which had until
then been tied up in physical development processes and manifest themselves again in the change of teeth are released for
action in mental development processes. Imagination and memory
are called into play and expanded in the process of interaction
which has already been described.

In the first three school years, practical learning - as
indeed all learning at the Hibernia School - is essentially

influenced by rhythm and beat. The object of the children's activity is not set as a task; they become aware of it in the course of execution. One activity of this kind has been described in paragraph 2.3.2.

In those years, artistic activities, such as training of finger skill in flute playing, careful handling of water colours in painting, and particularly drawing of shapes, should also be seen as practical education. The shape to be drawn, for instance, is first run by the children, then outlined in the air with a great sweep of the arms before it is drawn on a sheet of paper with a thick crayon. This form born of motion is finally raised to the level of consciousness when the children are called on to draw its mirror image, as an exercise in symmetry.

The objective is always to train the children's hands. Skill is a manifestation of practical consciousness. To guide the children in such a manner that they become aware of the potential of their hands is not only an important step in practical education but also in their development towards conceptual thinking. The fact that children really grasp only what they have first done themselves is obvious and underlies the entire educational conception of the Hibernia School. It is also the reason why from the very start tools and materials should be handled correctly. As all tools have been developed out of practical reasoning, using them has a direct effect on reasoning power.

In Grade 3 the children learn something about baking bread, house building and agriculture through direct engagement in such work (see 2.3.4 and 2.3.5). Once again they learn by imitation, by being given the opportunity of comprehending and grasping through practical participation. But at the same time their understanding of the interrelationship of man and nature is aroused. Such lessons have a key function, for they lay the foundation for far-reaching learning development. By getting to know a work process step by step in performing it themselves, their comprehension derives not merely from looking on or imagining but is enriched by all kinds of experience and committed activity. Such comprehension gives them the confidence that they will gradually be able to understand other matters in the bewildering diversity of their environment.

During the fourth to sixth school year (age 10-12) the children begin to become more aware of themselves as being distinct from their surroundings. Their spiritual life turns more inward, enabling them to see the object of their activities as something outside themselves and the activity as an entire process.

To support this development, new materials are introduced. Clay and wood have a more distinctive character than textiles and offer more resistance (2.3.7, clay modelling and wood carving). The activities also grow steadily more demanding. Handling the carving knife in Grade 5 requires great care and correct use of the tool, sewing dolls and soft toy animals in Grade 6 (2.3.8) calls for accuracy and attention down to the last detail.

Every new skill is taught step by step. In the first woodwork task, the so-called hand-carving, the wood is still held close to the body. Not until the children have progressed to making wooden animals with the rasp is the wood clamped into the vice and they take one step back from it, inwardly as well as physically. Even then, all the tasks set are still so selected that specific design and details are "felt out", discovered in the process of working. This helps the children to develop a feeling for proportions and to see the need for measuring. At first, when they make simple garments (2.3.6, knitting a pair of socks), they measure them against their own bodies. The next step is taken in woodwork. In making small articles of daily use, (a darning-egg, a cooking-spoon), they learn to determine the size and shape of the object and its purpose. While their own use of it, the form in which they themselves could most easily handle it, may still be a major consideration, they have to keep more closely to a given basic pattern, and this pattern dictates the sequence of the work process. It is important for the children at this stage to experience how purpose, the new aspect, combines with the already familiar one of beauty - how anything that serves a definite purpose is also aesthetically pleasing. They should at this stage develop a lasting desire to unite these two aspects in whatever they do.

Another activity based on direct perception and the resulting sensations is gardening, which commences at this learning stage in Grade 5 (2.3.9). What they have experienced in observing the annual cycle in plant life determines their actions.

The children's entire bodies are now involved in their practical activities. Whereas in the needlework lessons of the early grades it was mainly the fingers that were trained, clay-modelling and woodwork train the whole hand. They also demand a strong arm and a firm stance. Gardening requires even more. Many of the necessary activities cannot be properly performed unless the entire motor system is involved. This is useful for the children's further development. When they lose their natural smoothness of movement in the approaching phase of puberty the meaningful activities previously learnt help them to acquire a conscious and hence independent harmony of movement. Gymnastics and eurhythmy lessons (2.3.16 and 2.3.17) systematically support this development.

The educational problems connected with puberty primarily determine a learning provision in the following grades. Though the learning development occurring in Grades 7 and 8 still falls into the final part of the second period of life (age 7-14), it already contains elements of the characteristics of the third period (age 15-21). In the development of consciousness this can be seen in a growing understanding of causality and awareness of perspective and the spatial dimension. In practical education, the adolescents show a desire to place their activities into a social context. This is the time when they should learn to work not only for themselves or their immediate environment, but for the needs of others, that is to take on outside orders. However, they are not yet being trained for a specific occupation; their practical activities are merely meant to contribute to their all-round development. This new situation calls for a re-organization of the lessons. Up to then, practical activities were learnt in regular lessons, now they are taught in block periods, which offer an opportunity of designing each period as a project focussed on a particular task - an order - towards which the various learning steps are oriented. Most of these block periods are held in the school workshops in which the older students in training for a specialized occupation already carry out production work.

Special attention is paid at this learning stage to a thorough understanding of materials. The practical forestry period in Grade 7 serves the same purpose (2.3.10). One's own sometimes very strenuous experience in planting and nursing trees, felling and sawing wood teaches respect for the natural environment and the work of others.

Careful treatment of the material and respect for the work done by other people in preceding stages of a production process are indispensable if awareness of the social aspect of one's work is not to be lost in the situation of fragmented technical production. That is why woodwork in Grades 7 and 8 (2.3.12) starts with jobs in which the connection of the material with the tree can still be sensed, whereas such a connection is much more difficult to establish with the pressed wood used in more advanced cabinet work. In Grade 8 metal work is done for the first time. Copper sheeting has to be hammered into bowls or other containers (2.3.14). Owing to its hollow form, the container has a special significance at this learning stage. It corresponds to the spiritual processes of internalization characteristic of this age. That is also the reason for providing lessons in basket-weaving and carving of wooden bowls. Tasks are now set in which separate parts have to be joined together. This applies to needlework, where more difficult garments such as shirts, overalls and aprons are made, as well as to woodwork. Producing wooden toys that can be set moving by simple mechanisms (2.3.12) again anticipates the following period of life. The challenge to "invent", like the problem-solving group activities during construction, trains the practical imagination which is already beginning to develop. Though at this stage a model, be it an object or the teacher's skill, still directs the work, the details of construction have to be "re-invented" by joint efforts, and "the right way of doing it" shown by the teacher is "tested" in experiments so that it may be applied in the conviction that it really is the best. The teacher is now seen as an expert whose advice is sought and carries authority.

Since gardening, wood- and copper-work, sewing, basket-weaving and other manual activities are increasingly oriented by their specific purpose, thus taking on the nature of craft training, practice in the arts must be continued separately. This is done by providing block period lessons for the various arts and introducing techniques that require intensive practice (2.4.12).

The conception of the further practical education is now based on the characteristics of the third period of life (age 15-21), when the nature of the motivation for learning changes. Previously, motivation was generated by the teacher's example; now it springs from objective necessities imposed by facts and processes. The young people's growing powers of thought and judgement call for tasks that can be solved by reason. The adolescent now wants to direct his work by his own insights. He wants to see that it serves a purpose, and why he should do it in a particular way. Answers to such questions, demanded more radically in this than any later development phase, are given most effectively by the practical courses. They also relieve inhibitions peculiar to this age. For, in the process of finding his identity the adolescent needs criteria and standards which are objective, i.e. independent of the teacher. Such criteria are given him by his practical activities in that a successful piece of work must be usable; it must match the parts made by the other members of his team, as decided in previous discussion; and it must strictly conform to agreed measurements. The steel rule shows indisputably whether or not he has kept to these measurements; he can correct mistakes himself and obtains an objective indication of his abilities or shortcomings.

These abilities must also be acquired step by step. Practice is therefore given in planning of team-work and in evaluation, and before the pupils learn to work from given technical drawings they make their own. In Grades 9 and 10 these learning processes are initiated by elementary practice in work of a more technical nature, but also by more advanced craft-work. This culminates in gardening, cabinet-work and working at the forge. For instance, one basic experience appropriate to the phase of puberty is transmitted by working at the forge: the experience that it is possible to control one's strength, and that this can be done most successfully when one has found one's own working rhythm (2.4.7 and 2.4.5).

From the archetypal activity at the forge, in which he is still wholly involved, the adolescent advances to metal-work which demands increasing detachment. The way now leads from locksmith's work, where he has to adhere to specifications, to machine operation (2.4.14) where he controls a machine by adjusting and checking it but acts more as an "observer". The detachment needed at this stage of elementary technical education is also developed by the control of energy (2.4.10, electrical work) and of chemical processes (2.4.11, chemistry). Coping with unforeseen circumstances is learnt in a manner appropriate to this development phase in courses on games for children, first aid and domestic science. The mathematics and surveying block period (2.4.6) brings home the difficulty of applying theoretical knowledge to practice. It also provides immediate experiences of the siginificance and rules of group work.

During the 11th and 12th school year a desire for social responsibility develops. The adolescent wants to feel that he is needed. As this feeling is most strongly experienced in helping human beings in need of assistance, all pupils do practical work in Grade 11 (2.5.2 and 2.5.3). The training period in neighbouring factories provides the experience that working competence makes it possible to assume responsibility under industrial working conditions (2.5.4).

In order to enhance the adolescents' creative ability and to counterbalance the specialization necessary in vocational education, advanced courses in artistic craft-work (book-binding, metal-work, laying of mosaics) are offered, and art studies (singing, instrument playing, clay modelling, stone sculpturing) are continued.

Finally, the certificate examination gives every candidate an opportunity of showing that he has acquired the competence to produce something useful (2.6.7).

The foregoing summary descripiton of practical education in the Hibernia School would be incomplete if it failed to mention the physical training provided by eurhythmy and gymnastics and the continuous articulation of developments in practical learning with those of cognitive learning. Eurhythmy and gymnastics (2.3.16 and 2.3.17) have a basic function for all other kinds of learning at every learning stage. An elaboration of this statement would exceed the scope of this book. The interaction between cognitive and psycho-motor development is, however, illustrated in the following section.

### 3.4.4 *Possibilities of integrating theoretical and practical learning*

The significance of practical education not only for motor development, but also, and especially, for cognitive development has already been emphasized. In recent literature and discussions on educational policy the possibility of utilizing this interaction in a novel, dynamic way of promoting ability has given rise to a demand for an integration of theoretical and practical learning. In the following, the special form in which this demand is reflected in the conception of the Hibernia School will be described in a review and summary of the relevant information contained in Chapter 2. Attention is drawn to two central points:

1) Which particular cognitive developments are directly facilitated by practical learning?
2) How can the contents of theoretical and practical learning be integrated?

It has already been said that skill, which the initial stage of the practical course of education at the Hibernia School aims to develop, is a manifestation of practical consciousness. This practical consciousness has its primary root in an *increased power of observation*. The working hand must feel out the specific nature of the material (2.3.7). The movements of the arm and the tool must be perceived, internally by the sense of balance and motion, externally by the eye, and all changes brought about in the process of working must be observed in such a manner that they will guide the continuation of the process. As already stated, such cultivation of the senses manifested in skill governs all tasks given in the early grades. Exact factual description of the work process in Grade 7 raises the powers of observation to the level where processes and interactions can be comprehended (2.4.10). In the higher grades of the practical course, accurate measuring and observance of measurements play an increasingly important part, and the training of the power of perception is extended to precise observation.

Another field of cognitive development is the *training of judgement*. This training can be quite naturally combined with a practical course of education. Any judgement is based on comparison; it states whether, and in which respect, two things agree. In practical work judgement functions as an evaluation of the activity and its end product, i.e. of a concrete, objectively given reality. Such judgement is first applied in Grade 5 when the children check whether a sock fits (2.3.6), whether a toy animal has the right shape (2.3.8), whether the handle of a planting-stick made in the woodwork lessons lies well in the hand. In the upper grades the judgement processes become increasingly abstract. They now concern the function of the product (2.3.12) and later the functionality of the work process, observance of necessary norms, time limits, etc.

In this training the pupils gain immediate experience of the interrelationship of thought and action. Every thought translated into activity is tested by comparing the idea with the result. Thus their developing thinking capacity is constantly tested and corrected by practical reality. The evolving thought patterns, fact-oriented and close to real life, facilitate the learner's integration into social processes because he has acquired the habit of thinking of himself as an objective factor to be taken into account in his judgements.

The *capacity for conceptual thought* lies on yet another, higher level of cognitive development. It also can be directly fostered by practical education in a fundamental way linked with the young person's overall development.

The process of abstraction should first be practised by him in analyzing his own work. If he learns to understand the laws governing the work he has done, a way of thought which remains fact-related despite its abstractness will become second nature to him. Such practice may start with evaluating together with the instructor a mistake that has been made, for instance by discussing why a drill-bit broke, why a material became too brittle, why the product did not conform to specifications (2.4.14). If the right method is applied, any theme coming up in practical work or material study lends itself to such mental evaluation and cognitive penetration of personal experiences. The objective is to enable the young person when he enters the stage of technical production to understand in advance the procedure and conditions of an entire production process in order to be in a position to carry out his specific job with insight into the whole, and hence with self-determination. With this goal in view, planning and evaluation are practised at all stages of the practical course of education. Again this is done step by step: at first, for instance in gardening and woodwork, it relates only to some individual work phases; later, for instance in making the examination piece, the entire work is done independently (2.6.7).

Self-observation, self-evaluation and the capacity to take responsibility are characteristics of personal expansion. As has been shown, they are the results of a cognitive development facilitated and promoted by a practical education course.

The contents of academic and practical learning are most directly articulated in Vocational Studies (2.4.15). In addition to the domains of production and material study these include vocational mathematics and drawing as well as social studies. Up to and including the first semester of Grade 11, the Vocational Study lessons are of a more general nature and the whole class takes part in them. The contents correspond to those of the practical education course, which is also of a general kind. After the pupils have decided on the future field of occupation, the Vocational Study lessons are divided and each pupil attends those dealing with his speciality.

The objective of preparing the learner for comprehending and evaluating the experiences he makes in his practical activities dictates a continuous articulation of vocational studies and practical lessons. The temporal sequence of this method varies. Spatial thinking and spatial expression are progressively developed, starting from artistic exercises in light and shade drawing (shadows and the use of shadowing to give a three-dimensional appearance) via perspective and geometry (2.4.12) to application in the work process (ability to produce and read technical drawings), whereas personal experience of division of labour, workers' participation (or lack of it) or the implications of a separation of planning and executive competencies in an industrial production process, is acquired before the relevant problems and insights are worked out in the Social Studies and Economics lessons (2.6.4). The task of producing mechanical toys (2.3.12) links up with a Physics block period in which the basic types of motion and the mechanical means of motion transmission and transformation are discussed.

To ensure that the Vocational Studies are always linked with practical application, and thus to obtain a basis for articulation of academic and practical learning, these lessons are largely given by the teachers responsible for the practical courses. What the workshop teacher has explained, put into the context of experiences or dealt with by a problem-solving approach in a concrete situation at the workbench, in front of the machine tool, in the laboratory or school garden, is developed into wider insights in the Vocational Study lessons, and these insights in turn become ready-to-hand knowledge that is applied in the work process.

It is well-founded experience that such continuous interconnection has a very beneficial effect. Again and again it has been observed that adolescents, who enter the Hibernia School in the 9th or 10th Grade totally unwilling to learn, at odds with any intellectual learning, become interested in learning after a few months and make progress also, and especially, in academic learning areas. Furthermore, children with considerable learning handicaps who enter the Hibernia School in the early grades and are carried along by the class develop a progressive capacity for cognitive learning commensurate with their growing independence in the practical education course.

It is expected that a young person who has been able to attain independence with the help of the elementary approach described, who has learnt to act out of insight into facts, into his own personality and his environment and to relate these factors to each other, will have the capacity for further development. For he has been rendered capable not only of accepting, and even feeling a need for, new ideas appropriate to his age, but also of adapting them to real life so that they can be realized in individual or societal development. This requires a lifelong learning process in which ideas and action mutually correct and advance each other. It is learning from the reality of life and for life.

### 3.4.5 *The principle of ability promotion and its effect on achievement*

A question frequently mooted in the general discussion about educational policy as well as in deliberations on the pedagogical approach of the Hibernia School concerns the relationship between learning and achievement in cases where the idea of ability promotion is the determining element in the conception of education. Particular points needing clarification are the role played in the life of society by school certificates (leaving certificates, qualifications), the functions assigned to them and the justification for such functions in view of the actual information conveyed by this certification system. As an adequate investigation of these problems would far exceed the scope of this book, the answer to the above question will be limited to an outline of the way in which the performance of the young is fostered by the methodological approach of Rudolf Steiner Schools and in particular by the special form this approach has taken in the conception of the Hibernia School. This outline should demonstrate that there is no contradiction between ability promotion and achievement, because ability to achieve adequate performances is a major goal of educational promotion. It may also be said that current school practice is highly unsuitable for comprehensive achievement promotion, the more so as achievements have become an instrument of selection.

The general dissatisfaction with an "achievement society", in which access to training opportunities for vital professions, such as the medical profession, depends on final marks obtained in school subjects, is countered by Waldorf school education with its lucid and consistent concept. The demands it makes on the pupils can be met at every age and by every individual ability constellation. These demands relate equally to intellectual, manual and social capacities. The broader and more versatile the learning provision - and in the Hibernia School it is both -, the more opportunities are given to the pupil to develop, to prove himself and to acquire new abilities in various fields.

It will be obvious that a practical education course with its very concrete and delineable tasks is especially suited to facilitate such aided achievement development. It offers the best opportunities for consistent application of an approach which promotes individual achievement and where motivation does not arise from fear and ambition as it does in the current general practice dominated by the selection principle. But what other kind of motivation can be substituted?

Every human being has an innate desire to learn and to develop through learning. This is most evident in small children; it can also be perceived in full strength at every later stage of childhood and adolescence if the young grow up in an educational climate which facilitates achievement and makes them aware of their development. It must, however, be recognized that inner learning motivation changes with the various phases of development.

In the description of these phases it has been shown that at pre-school age and in the first few years of schooling, the child learns entirely through its attachment to the educator; first through its urge to imitate, then through psychological communication with the educator in whom it seeks an authority. Later, this personal authority is supplemented by the authority of matter. The piece of work the learner has to produce assumes authoritative force, he wants to be able to do it himself and to learn everything that is necessary for the purpose. This new orientation is taken into account whenever learning matter is presented in the form of projects. It finds expression in the new way in which the pupils keep their block period diaries which now assume an individual character; their artistic activities (e.g. designing a wooden or metal bowl or preparing a dramatic performance) offer good opportunities for such individualization. But it is the practical courses that respond best to this kind of motivation.

It must, however, be realized that learning and achievement motivation arising from commitment to their own work, though it represents an important step towards independence, is not in itself sufficient to enable the young to meet the demands of a technical civilization. The special significance of art and craft work lies in the fact that in the work he has produced the learner confronts himself. This prepares him for the pubertal phase when he wants to see himself objectively, to recognize the reasons for his actions and his learning. To aid this process, Grade 7 pupils are given work for which there is an objective necessity (2.3.10); Grade 9 pupils have to produce, not a complete object but a part for which an outside order has been received, and which must therefore conform to specifications as it must in industrial production. At that stage the adolescents should learn everything they need to execute an order responsibly within a specific production context; but they should also learn all that is necessary to do something in which they are personally interested. Learning out of personal interest and learning for tasks originating from the society generates motivation, a motivation which - if it were taken into account in the learning provision and organization of our educational system - would so increase the self-direction of the young in their learning and performance that they would be capable of participating with responsibility and initiative in building up a technical culture in all its aspects.

a) Evaluation

From an overview of what a child can already do, how he can do it and how he acquired that ability, his specific developmental type should be recognized and should serve as a basis for an evaluation of whether the progress evidenced by his achievements is adequate or needs special stimulation. Ability research has shown how widely individual learning developments differ in respect of speed and predominant areas. An appraisal of achievement is, therefore, meaningful and pedagogically justified only when it is made on the basis of an all-round, complex learning development that has been facilitated by a corresponding range of learning provision, and when it considers not only the state already reached but also the development potential indicated by the achievement profile.

In the Hibernia School, achievement, i.e. the extent to which the targets of a school year have been reached, is therefore not expressed in figures (marks) but in a characterization of the progress made in each subject; in the case of inadequate progress the causes are sought and possible remedies suggested. Unless an appraisal is set within the total framework of the individual's nature and circumstances it has little or no validity.

In the first eight grades the class teacher gives the parents in addition a characterization of the pupil's overall development with suggestions of possible supporting measures they might take, such as music lessons, cultivation of friendships, etc. In the upper grades and in the leaving certificates this complex appraisal is supplemented by achievement marks in order to give the youths a possibility of comparing their performances with those of others who go to schools where the marking system is used.

More important than the form in which the appraisal is communicated is the discussion of the pupils in the conferences where the principles of ability promotion emerge more distinctly, as will have been gathered from sections 1.3, 2.2.3, 2.2.4 and 2.8.3.c). Some of the main aspects of this appraisal may be summarized as follows:

1) Achievement in a particular subject is always assessed in terms of the pupil's development. This may be very evident in his commitment to the lessons. Within a pupil's overall development there may, however, be retarding phases which must be understood individually.

2) Lack of motivation may thus have various reasons, and discovering them may already be of help to the child. For, as observation of small children shows, every human being has an innate desire to learn and to develop through learning. If the school does not succeed in responding to the changes in individual motivation, the objective of promoting the pupil cannot be realized.

b) <u>Leaving examinations</u>

The goal of achievement promotion may be formulated as follows:
- Everything possible should be done to encourage the child and adolescent to fulfil himself and to give him the confidence that he will be able to master any step in learning and achievement because he can be certain of aid and support from the teacher.

Given this goal, every effort must be made not to vitiate it by an inappropriate examination procedure. The Hibernia

School has, therefore, endeavoured to devise a procedure which, though original, would produce results fully comparable with those of the general examination practice. The latter, and the qualifications connected with it, are rooted in the principle of selection which is contrary to the understanding of man inspiring the Waldorf schools. It takes its orientation from the current employment system, the qualifications structure of which has the hierarchical pattern and the dependencies of a rigid Taylorism with its socially destructive implications.

The leaving examinations of the Hibernia School also compare the pupils' achievements. But they are so designed as to provide each pupil with opportunities for individual expansion.

The *certificate of apprenticeship examination* is based on real work tasks. However, the learners, counselled by the workshop instructors, choose their tasks themselves, and when their choice has been approved by the examination committee, they prepare and execute them themselves. In the oral examination each pupil has to show that he is also capable of explaining what he has done by himself, or maybe jointly with a classmate, and of stating and justifying the reasons for his planning and execution. Every approved examination task is commensurate with the capacity of the pupil concerned. In accordance with the principle that a learner should only be set tasks he is capable of doing, he now has to assess his own capacity, i.e. he has to choose a task that lies within his abilities but at the same time gives him a chance of showing the best he can do (2.6.7). He is thus offered an opportunity of testing his self-evaluation objectively. At the same time, passing the examination implies that his future colleagues consider him capable of participating responsibly in the employment system of his chosen occupation. So designed, the examination becomes a justified, even a motivating link in his learning development, and one that respects and reinforces the self-direction he has acquired.

Finding an appropriate form for the acquisition of qualifications entitling to entry into institutions of further or higher education is more difficult. It seems very doubtful whether firm forecasts of future learning developments can be made on the basis of the progress and success of a completed one. An attempt has, however, been made to design these examinations also in such a manner that they correspond to the preceding cognitive learning development. A written examination paper is set at the end of a period during which the learners had a chance of studying in depth the special field concerned and the methods employed in this field. This paper is not so much intended to show how much knowledge a pupil can readily reproduce, but rather whether he is able to comprehend a problem and to solve it by applying a suitable method. The oral examination is handled in a similar way. The learners are told ten days in advance whether, and in which subject, they will be orally examined, and as there are no lessons during these ten days they have time for thorough preparation.

Another characteristic of the Hibernia School examinations is that qualification for further or higher education can only be acquired in combination with a vocational leaving examination. (4) Both examinations are taken either simultaneously or one after the other, in which case the vocational one always comes first.

The conditions currently prevailing in the society, in particular its employment and further or higher education systems (university level institutions, technical schools and other forms of adult education) are always being kept in view. For self-fulfilment implies that the young person should be able to utilize his innovative potential within the existing social reality.

A persisting problem is that, measured by the contemporary form of our social order, Hibernia School learners are "overqualified". There is no system that would correspond to their learning competence by offering equal lifelong educational opportunities to all; their capacity for self-responsible action finds no outlet in the basic occupations of the present employment system; their desire for direct participation in all societal processes still has to create the forms of society that will make it possible. However, these are problems that lie beyond the responsibility of an educational institution such as the Hibernia School. They will be taken up again in the concluding paragraphs of this book.


3.5  Outcomes of training in learning competence. Curricula vitae of ex-pupils

It will have been obvious that at every step this book contains information on how learning competence can be mediated. This mediation of learning competence is the central concern of Rudol Steiner pedagogy. It may be said that its special form as evolved in the Hibernia School makes a significant contribution to this fundamental requirement. Chapter 1 of this book has described how, in its search for a new, contemporary form of training for working life, the school became aware that its principal task should be to mediate learning competence as the basis for lifelong vocational learning.

When a new educational concept is being developed it is imperative that there should be a check on whether the envisaged goals are being attained. For that reason the Hibernia School has kept in contact with its ex-pupils from an early date. Moreover, it has carried out inquiries at local labour authorities and larger commercial enterprises in the area in order to obtain information on the further development of its former pupils. It was found that these were appreciated by employers because they were able to adjust quickly to new situations and to take on responsibility. These qualities are frequently combined with considerable vertical as well as horizontal mobility, although the Hibernia School especially aims at expanding the knowledge and skills of those working in basic occupations.

As it has not yet been possible to process the data that have been collected on nearly a thousand ex-pupils, no statistical information will be given here. Instead, four curricula vitae are presented which may indicate the wide spectrum of possible further vocational learning. While these four case histories are, of course, the results of individual initiative, they may be considered representative insofar as they cover the four major occupational areas (professional work, development aid, trades, kindergarten teaching) for which the Hibernia School is providing a training.

The following report has been chosen as an example of an ex-pupil who acquired further qualifications in his chosen occupation:

> When I had completed my training as a lathe-turner in 1960, I started work immediately. Being an orphan I had to earn my own living and could not go in for further education. In my first employment, in a mining company, I had no opportunity of learning anything new. But I wanted to develop my own ideas, take decisions and create something myself, work on a project. I succeeded in finding a more congenial job in the experimental workshop of a factory producing pneumatic tools. There I was

able to consolidate and increase my knowledge by developing my own work-processes, work-preparation and techniques. I was assigned to pilot production, that is new constructions the measurements and constructional details of which had to be developed in the workshop before they could go into serial production. In this work, where form had to be balanced with utility, the knowledge of design and of welding I had acquired in my training proved very useful. I also had opportunities of cooperating with constructors, engineers and heads of departments and learnt to appreciate the value of tests at all stages of development of a product. Some advice I was able to offer was accepted. For economic reasons I had to leave this firm, but obtained another very interesting job in the production control of a chemical factory. My field of work was metrology and automatic control technology. Though this was entirely new to me, I was soon able to work independently. For instance, I constructed a new high-pressure synthesis control station to which four high-pressure chambers and several subsidiary lines had to be connected. It was important that the recorders, indicators and controls on the front panel should be so arranged that the operators could easily read and operate them, and that the lines from the measuring devices to the station should be easy to follow so that any defect could be quickly located. I may say that thanks to my imagination having been constantly trained in all my previous work I succeeded in meeting all these requirements. The necessary cooperation with planning personnel was also satisfactory for both sides.

In the meantime I had married and had a son who was approaching school age. I enrolled him in the Hibernia School as I wished him to receive the same practical and artistic education I had had and found valuable in later life. I began to take an interest in the parents' cooperation with the school and decided to become more involved in these activities. When my son entered Grade 1, the parents of that grade elected me a member of the Parents' Association, from which I was subsequently elected to Parents Advisory Council. I now had to familiarize myself with the foundations of Waldorf school education, recruit new parents and find out what the parents were mainly concerned about and what were the real problems in order to incorporate these into the programmes for the meetings. In this work I learnt a lot about dealing with people, though I also experienced disappointments when I did not succeed in motivating the parents as I had wished.

Since, owing to the diversity of my work, I have now acquired sufficient knowledge and experience, I am at present taking a masters' course, in the hope that this will give me access to positions involving social problems within my occupation, either in the field of personnel welfare or of training of the young.

The question is often asked whether pupils aiming for university studies need an education in art and craft. The following report has been chosen as an example of a pupil who from the start intended to go to university but nevertheless underwent the art and craft training at what was then the Hibernia Education and Training Centre:

I was already 16 years old when I entered the Hibernia School in 1954, after six years attendance at a grammar school. I intended to become an engineer, and my parents and I felt that a broader education including craft training would be a better foundation for that career. However, at the Hibernia School I discovered my artistic abilities and decided that industrial design would presumably suit me better.

On leaving school I first took several training courses. Then I attended a school for engineers, where I obtained a qualification entitling me to enter university without the *Abitur*. After working for some time at an electro-technical company as an engineer developing electric kitchen appliances, I had the good luck to be accepted, out of over hundred applicants, by the Design College at Ulm. But I left it soon after because it was going to close down. In partnership with a designer I then set up my own enterprise. I had already registered a patent; now I designed and developed unconventional types of such articles as a snow blower, a set of furniture, tripods for movie cameras and grills.

In a very short time I had earned enough money to finance a course of studies at the Technical University. My thesis, with the out-of-the-way title "Aesthetic Proportions of Technical Products" was published in abbreviated form in several technical journals.

In order to gain practice in assuming responsibility I took a course of training as an engine-driver with the German Federal Railways and drove all kinds of train for some four months.

With the aid of a scholarship I went to the University of California to study a variety of subjects such as sculpture, methodology of architecture and design, ergonomics, operations research, etc. which I needed for the occupation I had in mind. After graduating as a master of science I considered various job opportunities and finally settled on the German Federal Railways. First I worked in the planning group, where I drew up fundamental studies on the planning of an inter-city network and other large projects. Then I took postgraduate training in mechanical and electric railway engineering, passed the second state examination and was put in charge of a railway marshalling-yard with nearly 400 engine drivers and other personnel. After several months of this hard operational work I returned to designing. I joined the staff of the Design Center at Munich which had just been established by the German Federal Railways for the purpose of designing railway vehicles, buildings and information material. At present I am head of the department of vehicle design. In cooperation with other members of the center I design those parts of engines and coaches which are directly visible to and are used by the public and by operators.

I have also travelled fairly extensively both within and outside Europe. The possibilities and, above all, the ability to work responsibly in various fields offer a grand opportunity of widening one's horizons.

The next report illustrates how craft and technical education can lead someone who aims at university study to further learning in new areas and to a healthy attitude to life:

When I was 14 years of age and had had 8 years' education at primary plus lower secondary level, I was uncertain as to what to do next. My interest in technical matters suggested a craft-technical training. On the other hand, I felt a need for a better and deeper general education. As the Hibernia School seemed to offer a way out of this conflict I entered it, leaving the choice of a future occupation aside for the time being.

The educational structure of the Hibernia School with its combination of academic and practical education really answered my problem. I needed the practical side to balance the theoretical side and vice versa. This is still the case today. After the basic practical education it was easier for me to choose an occupation because I had been given opportunities of finding out what I liked and what suited me best. Furthermore, a desire to continue learning had developed in the course of this education. The question of whether I had made the right choice in deciding to become an elctrical engineer was no longer of such vital importance. Four years after entering the Hibernia School I passed the leaving examination and now had the option of going to an engineering college or preparing for university entrance.

As I enjoyed learning at the Hibernia School, I decided to stay on for the *Abitur* course. Education was now mostly academic. But it did include a 6 week course of practical social training for work with mentally handicapped children. My experiences gained in this course, reinforced by the ideas of the student movement, influenced my decision to register as a conscientious objector to military service. During the years in the *Fachkolleg* (Social and Technical Section). and especially while I was working on my examination paper on calculation in the binary system, the idea of studying mathematics or computer science took shape.

After the final secondary school leaving examination and approval of my application for exemption from military service on the grounds of conscientious objection I had to choose a civilian service in lieu. My urge to see and experience something new led me to select development aid. I went to Zambia for two years, where I was responsible for the theoretical and practical training of 18 apprentice electricians at a polytechnical school. In addition, I gave evening courses for unskilled workers to prepare them for the examination qualifying them as skilled electricians. Despite doubts about the usefulness of this development aid work I have never regretted those two years, for they were development aid for myself. They gave me an opportunity of assuming responsibility and proving to myself and to others that I was competent to carry it. Besides, I learnt three important things: improved knowledge of human nature, more differentiated judgement, and greater self-confidence.

After returning from Zambia I started studying mathematics and computer-science. At present I am working on a thesis. At the same time I have a job as a computer programming assistant, and this more practical activity provides a counterbalance to the theoretical work. When I have completed my studies I hope to get a position in the border areas of data processing and medicine or data processing and education. My wife and I would also like to work abroad for a time.

Finally, a report by an ex-girl-pupil will perhaps show how responsible assumption of a social task increases opportunities for further learning and hence for developing new ideas and putting them into practice:

After four years at a girls grammar school I was tired of school. Vocational guidance officers drew my parents' and my attention to the Hibernia School, and in 1962 I entered it in Grade 9. My initial scepticism faded when I found that my class teacher understood my problems and tried to help me solve them. This experience also encouraged me to drop my reserve towards other people.

At the time I intended to become an interior decorator. But the practical carpentry period made me realize that this was not the right career for me. On the other hand, I much enjoyed the practical kindergarten and domestic science training periods. So I chose the social and educational area of occupation. Work in the children's home, the infants' ward at the hospital and the kindergarten enhanced my interest in this training. In 1966 I passed the child-nursing and technical school entrance examinations and intended to continue studying at the Hibernia School up to the final examination qualifying for university entrance. But I soon missed the practical activities and noticed that without them I was less able to learn theory. I then left the school and took a six month practical probation course, largely in a day home for mentally handicapped children. This work gave me an insight into a variety of activities and case histories. It also included craft-work with older handicapped children in the workshop of the home. The Head and I devised individual craft and speech therapy programmes which I was allowed to carry out independently. This task suited me so well that I stayed on at the home when the probation period was over.

In 1973 I attended the pre-school teacher class the Hibernia School had in the meantime established. In the course of that year we were informed of a new project, a children's day home which would eventually provide full-day care for 110 children ranging in age from four months to 14 years. I took an immediate interest in this task. Two of my classmates, one younger ex-Hibernia-pupil and myself formed a group to develop the new project. A first concept of collegiate management of the new institution was worked out in many discussions with the sponsors. Afterwards we met regularly to draw up an operational programme down to details of room design, furniture, crockery and toys. In order to create a warm atmosphere, we wanted the rooms to be half-panelled. The architect considered this an unnecessary expenditure; besides, it was new to him that matters such as these should be determined by pedagogical considerations. Eventually it was agreed that we should do the panelling ourselves. This meant a lot of extra work, which had to be done in the evenings because we were still working in other institutions. Gradually the architect came to understand our pedagogical viewpoints and helped us in selecting furniture, paint, etc. Other items of decoration or equipment we purchased or made ourselves. At weekends each of us collected stones, tree roots, fir cones, shells, etc., because natural materials are important for kindergarten education.

Having got to know each other well through these joint preparatory activities, we were then able to decide on the distribution of functions. Each of us took over one area, with one of the other three acting as deputy. After two years everyone was to take over a different area.
These function areas are:
Personnel: Service schedules, leave, sickness reports, cleaning personnel.
Technical: Mail, repairs, keys, purchases, accounts.
Legal/educational: Responsibility to the Board of the home, health office, insurance agencies, contact with parents' representatives.
Public relations: Visitors, contact with authorities, reports to hospital magazine and daily paper.

Many of these matters were dealt with by all of us in the weekly general conference. In these conferences new colleagues were also familiarized with our collegiate style of management, which makes it possible for everybody to identify with the overall task of the home and his own work within it, and to take initiative. Through this type of management my colleagues and myself learn to see ourselves as co-workers towards a common goal, to become more flexible towards our own views and to obtain the stimulus to new thought.

## 3.6 Applicability of the Hibernia School concept to the national school system

### 3.6.1 *Staff, parents, financing*

A major consideration throughout the step by step development process of the Hibernia School concept which has been described in Chapter 1 has been its applicability to the national educational system. The following review of the composition of the School's teaching staff, the social background of pupils' parents and its financial aspects may bear this out.

The teaching staff of the Hibernia School differs markedly from the usual contemporary pattern. Its members come from all social strata; a considerable number originate from the very stratum whose disadvantages the new educational approach is intended to overcome. Many have worked in other occupations before entering the educational field; they were engineers, merchants, technicians or skilled workers, artists, scholars or housewives. Those who had already been teachers served in every conceivable kind of school or institution in the present educational system. Nevertheless, all are equal members of the teaching staff of the Hibernia School, and all have equal responsibility for their own task as well as for the whole school. This kind of broad-based staff composition can be easily adopted by the general education system with its wide social range. Indeed, it must be adopted if a new learning reality is to be established. What is new in our approach does not need *special* ability. It can be learnt. The only indispensable qualifications are enthusiasm for education and readiness to continue learning.

The position is similar in regard to the parents of Hibernia School pupils. As already mentioned, they belong to all social strata of our society and represent the social and employment structure of the region. But they also must learn to develop active commitment; their own experiences at school and other public institutions have not generated it. Willingness of both parents and teaching personnel to act as partners in the common educational task, to make a joint effort to discover what is needed to foster the learning development of the children and to complement each other's educational actions, is a fundamental requirement of a new type of school. It is an important experience made by the Hibernia School that this readiness can be aroused in all population strata and that the necessary abilities can be acquired through learning.

As regards the financial aspect, it has already been stated in paragraph 2.8.1 that the costs of the Hibernia School are no higher than those of the various existing learning institutions that must be attended to achieve the same level of education. General acceptance of the educational principles of the Hibernia School would signify a step on the way to real equality of educational opportunity by offering *every* young person learning provision which would enable him to fulfil his all-round human potential.

Again, the experience of the Hibernia School shows what considerable sacrifices parents, particularly those from the less well-to-do population groups, are prepared to make for the sake of their children's education. If they let them remain at the school instead of sending them to the conventional type of apprenticeship, they not only lose the state allowance for apprentices, but have to make financial contributions to cover that part of the school's expenditure which is not covered by state grants. Their willingness to do so is another important indication of the wide applicability of the Hibernia School model.

3.6.2 *Preconditions for adopting the Hibernia School concept*

The history of the Hibernia School shows that it has been a continuous - and still continuing - learning process for all concerned. So must the adoption of the concept by other educational institutions be a continuous learning process for all concerned. For, although general applicability has been constantly kept in view, the outcomes of the Hibernia School development have been evolved to meet an educational and societal situation which, while typical of the present state of development of our age, may differ in some respects from that of other institutions. They cannot, therefore, be simply handed on as universally effective recipes. Rather are they offered as suggestions, as examples of possible methods of institutionalizing the fundamental principle of ability promotion. How to adapt the outcomes presented in this book to the specific situation of other establishments and to the future development of society must be found out in a *development process* which has its own inherent conditions and follows a course that accords with these conditions. It must thus be *self-directed* and *self-responsible*.

To be successful, this development process must be a

*societal process* involving every educator - teacher or parent. The principle of ability promotion can only be realized when every educator is capable of implementing it. And he can only acquire this capability to the extent that he progresses in his own learning development.

This has institutional implications:

1) Since the new educational competence can only be developed in practising it, a *partnership situation* between teachers and parents is an essential precondition for transition to a system governed by the principle of ability promotion.

2) A second precondition is a *collegiate structure* which will engender a common consciousness and facilitate agreement on cooperative action.

3) To initiate the transition process there must be *readiness to discontinue all measures directed by the idea of selection*; furthermore, efforts should be made to supplement the existing learning provision step by step in accordance with the principle of all-round ability promotion, especially by *facilitating practical and social learning*.

4) Finally, the primary consideration in selecting learning provision and designing learning processes should be their *suitability for the development stage of the learners concerned*.

### 3.6.3 Reconsideration of the role of the state

When the Hibernia School was recognized as an experimental school and loosened its ties with the industrial company from which it had originated, it did not become a state institution but an independent school.

It has already been said earlier in this chapter that an education aiming to enable every young person to attain the autonomy of a fully mature human being can only be given by educators who are themselves in a position to act autonomously, that is with self-direction and self-responsibility. Equally, it has been argued that societal reform in keeping with the times must be a self-directed learning process desired and carried out by all concerned.

On these premises, what would be the role of the state vis-à-vis a network of self-administering educational institutions? Clearly, a state-controlled school is not the place where autonomous educational action can proceed unhindered in the sense described in this book, and that reforms of a whole system of such schools are difficult to implement should be evident from the statements made in the preceding section.

When early last century the state took over the school system, freeing it from the bonds of corporate or church patronage, this was a historically necessary step on the way to emancipation; but it did not take the further step of permitting unfettered self-administration of the schools by those immediately concerned. State control has resulted in a rigidly organized and monopolistic learning system.

What is needed is not a return of the schools to the private sector but greater involvement of the whole society in decision-making. This implies that the relationship between the state and society must be re-thought, and that new forms of direct participation in societal processes and corresponding new forms of societal institutions are developed. All these issues can only be very briefly mentioned in the present book, but they are inseparably bound up with the question of the applicability to the national system of the concept of education realized in the Hibernia School.

### 3.7 Prospects. Lifelong learning and the reform of society

If it is accepted that any societal reform is by its nature a learning process, then clearly the innovative potential of a modern society rests on the learning competence of all its members. Thus the question frequently asked whether our society is incapable of reform means, among other things, whether the current educational system generates and develops individual learning competence, and whether its structure permits the lifelong learning that should result from such competence. Anybody who desires a further development of society, who wants to contribute to making a reality of the ideas expressed in the Basic Law of the Federal Republic of Germany, in human rights conventions, etc., should, therefore, endeavour to change the educational system of his society into one that will mediate individual learning competence.

Measured by the reality of our contemporary society, those educated in this way are overqualified. But they have the competence to change the toatlity of societal processes in such a manner that they can adequately participate in them and realize themselves through this participation. This will then also apply to all institutions of further learning, now called university study and adult education. Significant proposals in this direction, for instance the OECD recommendation of "recurrent education", have already been made. A common feature of all such proposals is that they want to establish a new relationship between learning and work. Instead of learning everything they will need in later life en bloc before they enter working life, people should learn only as much as they will require to enter a work process. Thereafter, working life should be repeatedly interrupted by learning periods in which the experience they have already acquired is utilized to prepare them for other work areas or for assumption of higher positions in the same area. Besides, individual needs to build up new fields of interest and to consolidate existing ones should be met.

All proposals of this kind are, however, dependent on preceding learning developments in which general, all-round learning competence has been generated, as the Hibernia School concept aims to do. Such earlier development is imperative because

1) every member of society must have the individual competence, i.e. the readiness and ability for lifelong further learning;

2) this general will to learn and the readiness to change oneself in learning will provide the potential for realizing new societal institutions.

This is the special prospect of a reform process which, though meant to cover all aspects of societal life, starts with the learning system. For the learning process necessary to change that system cannot fail to affect all domains of society. What has been experienced and practised in the new forms of institutionalized partnership of parents, teachers and all others directly involved in the children's learning processes will help to create new forms of active participation, co-determination and co-responsibility in all other areas of societal life. The wish to contribute to this end has been the reason for establishing the Hibernia School. The hope of encouraging such developments has inspired the writing of this book.

## NOTES

(1) Steiner, Rudolf: *Anthroposophische Leitsätze*. GA 26, L. 1972.

(2) In *Aufsätze über die Dreigliederung des sozialen Organismus und zur Zeitlage, 1915-1921*. GA 24. Dornach 1961, p.83.

(3) See Steiner, Rudolf: *Nationalökonomischer Kurs*. GA 340. In 14 lectures R. Steiner gave to national economy students in 1922, he developed a socio-economic theory based on spiritual science, in the context of which he characterized the concept of work.

(4) An exception due to official regulations is the examination for entry to a College of Technology, for which only participation in practical training courses but no leaving certificate is required.

APPENDIX

SCHOOL REPORT

Gabriele, born 25th October 1955, has attended Grade 5 of the Hibernia School in the school year 1966/67.

Class teacher

Gabriele has continued to take a liveley and receptive interest in the lessons. She often participates actively and poses thoughtful questions. Her exuberant temperament does, however, also induce her to chat and play during the lessons. When admonished she is very sorry and tries to improve, but these efforts should have more lasting effect.

She gets on well with her classmates. Even when she has a quarrel, she can give in, and her cheerfulness helps her to achieve a quick reconciliation. Her relationship with the teacher is open and uninhibited.

It is to be hoped that in the next school year Gabriele will succeed better in giving undivided attention to the lessons. She will then be more successful in all subjects.

In German, the subject of story-telling was Greek mythology. Gabriele listened very intently and was happy to retell the stories, which she did very graphically. - She recites poems clearly and expressively, with inner involvement. - Her reading could be more fluent if she were calmer and avoided slips of the tongue. - In spelling she succeeds in overcoming her difficulties when she pays careful attention. - In grammar she learnt to differentiate between the active and passive form and to convert one into the other. Her syntax exercises were satisfactory.

In mathematics she is quite good at multiplication. She knows the four basic types of calculation and can use them efficiently. She solves simple rule-of-three problems correctly and can also work quite satisfactorily with decimals when she concentrates.

In history, Gabriele showed considerable interest. She wrote fine, substantial compositions. Her exercise book was neatly kept, often in very good handwriting.

In geography she participated most eagerly. This was also evident in her written work. She outlined maps correctly but ought to finish them more carefully and with better handwriting.

In botany Gabriele participated well and showed much interest. Her compositions were good in form and content. She kept her exercise book well. But she should always write and draw as well as she can when wants to.

Gabriele was very interested in zoology. She wrote quite graphic compositions, but the summaries seem a little careless. She should take more trouble with her handwriting and drawings.

For Gabriele:

> A poem by Goethe
>
> Sag es niemand, nur den Weisen,
> Weil die Menge gleich verhöhnet,
> Das Lebendige will ich preisen,
> Das nach Flammentod sich sehnet.
>
> Und so lang du das nicht hast,
> Dieses: Stirb und werde!
> Bist du nur ein trüber Gast
> Auf der dunklen Erde.
>
> (Translation)
>
> Tell nobody but the wise,
> The mob will only scoff,
> I want to praise all those alive
> Who yearn to die in flames.
>
> And until you have learnt this:
> To die and grow and rise
> You'll be but a sorry guest
> on the sombre earth.

From: *West-östlicher Divan.*

Your class teacher C. Pr.

## Specialist teachers

**Religion:** Gabriele's attention to the lessons varies considerably. She still insists on playing with all sorts of things and often disturbs the whole class by her fidgety behaviour and lack of concentration. If she developed more outward and inward discipline she could be a good scholar.

**English:** Gabriele has become steadier in her work. She has repeatedly endeavoured to improve her pronunciation and reading. In written work she could make greater efforts.

**Latin:** Gabriele must work harder and concentrate more. She will then enjoy Latin texts better and improve her knowledge. Her exercise books show neither diligence nor reliability.

**Music:** Gabriele can perform her pieces of flute music correctly. Her tone is soft and pure. She enjoys singing songs, has a good voice and pronounces the texts clearly.

**Painting/Drawing:** Gabriele has gradually improved her drawing of geometric exercises, but still requires greater ease and fluidity of line. Some of her free exercises have been quite good. In painting with colour she has produced many pretty pictures.

**Carving/Modelling:** Always pleasant and willing, Gabriele has taken an active part in the lessons. She has learnt to carve neatly. In rasping work she should now show more determination and concentration.

**Eurhythmy:** When her injured leg prevented her from joining in exercises, Gabriele watched them attentively. She can competently execute sound gestures with her arms and run rhythms and forms distinctively.

**Gymnastics:** To her great regret Gabriele was unable for some considerable time to participate in these lessons, which she normally does most enthusiastically.

Needlework: On the whole, Gabriele is still very playful and lacking in concentration. She could have done her knitted slippers a little more carefully. Though she very willingly helped to do work for the annual festival, she must make an effort to carry it out more successfully.

Gardening: Gabriele has shown much interest and industriousness in gardening work.


Date: 26th July, 1967

        Signature (class teacher)

Signature

(School Management)

        Signature

        (parent or person responsible for the pupil)

BIBLIOGRAPY

1) Books about Rudolf Steiner and his Work

ABENDROTH, Walter: *Rudolf Steiner und die heutige Welt. Ein Beitrag zur Diskussion um die menschliche Zukunft.* München: List Verlag, 1972. (List Taschenbücher 480).

HEMLEBEN, Johannes: *Rudolf Steiner in Selbstzeugnissen und Bilddokumenten.* Reinbek bei Hamburg: Rowohlt Taschenbuch Verlag, 1972. (rowohlts monographien 79).

RIHOUET-COROZE, S.: *Biographie de Rudolf Steiner.* Paris: Triades, 1973.

SHEPHERD, A.P.: *A Scientist of the Invisible.* London: Hodder and Stoughton, 1961.

WACHSMUTH, Gunther: *The Life and Work of Rudolf Steiner.* New York: Whittier Books, 1955.

2) Publications about Waldorf School Education

*Arbeiten und Lernen.* Berlin: Arbeitsstelle für Bildungsforschung, 1975. (Bd.4).

BAI, Sönke u.a.: *Die Rudolf Steiner Schule Ruhrgebiet: Leben, Lehren, Lernen in einer Waldorfschule. Eine freie Schule sieht sich selbst.* Reinbek bei Hamburg: Rowohlt Taschenbuch Verlag, 1976. (rororo 6985).

BARAVALLE, Hermann von: *The International Waldorf School Movement.* New York: St. George Publications, 1975.

"Berufsgrundbildungsjahr". *Schulmanagement.* (1974), Nr.6.

BILDUNGSMISSION DES DEUTSCHEN BILDUNGSRATES: *Zur Reform von Organisation und Verwaltung im Bildungswesen.* Bonn: Bundesdruckerei, 1973. (Deutscher Bildungsrat. Empfehlungen).

BILDUNGSKOMMISSION DES DEUTSCHEN BILDUNGSRATES: *Zur Neuordnung der Sekundarstufe II. Konzept für eine Verbindung von allgemeinem und beruflichem Lernen.* Bonn: Bundesdruckerei, 1974. (Deutscher Bildungsrat, Empfehlungen).

BLUME, Helmut: *Lehrlingsbildung als soziale Aufgabe. Versuche und Erfahrungen.* Stuttgart: Mellinger, 1963.

BRITSCHE, Hellmuth: "Das Bochumer Modell eines 9. Schuljahres". *Berufspädagogische Zeitschrift.* (1960), No.2/3.

CARLGREN, F.; KLINGBORG, A.: *Education towards Freedom.* Peredur, East Grinstead, Sussex, England: The Lanthorn Press, 1976.

EDMUNDS, L. Francis: *Rudolf Steiner Education.* London: Rudolf Steiner Press, 1962.

———: *Rudolf Steiner's Gift to Education.* London: Rudolf Steiner Press, 1975.

FINTELMANN, Klaus J.: *Ziel, Aufbau und Entstehung der Hiberniaschule.* Stuttgart: Freies Geistesleben, 1968. (Veröffentlichungen der Pädagogischen Forschungsstelle der Hiberniaschule, Heft 1. Menschenkunde und Erziehung 24).

———: *Die Hiberniaschule als Modell einer Gesamtschule des beruflichen Bildungsweges.* Stuttgart: Freies Geistesleben, 1968. (Veröffentlichungen der Pädagogischen Forschungsstelle der Hiberniaschule, Heft 2. Menschenkunde und Erziehung 24).

———: "Entstehung und Aufbau der Hiberniaschule". *Pädagogik heute.* (1969), Nr.1/2. (Sonderdruck).

FUCKE, Erhard: *Berufliche und allgemeine Bildung in der Sekundarstufe II. Ein Modell.* Stuttgart: Klett, 1976.

GLAS, Werner: *Speech Education in the Primary Grades of Waldorf Schools.* Wilmington, Delaware: Sunbridge College Press, 1974.

GRUNELIUS, Elizabeth: *Early Childhood Education and the Waldorf School Plan.* Englewood, New Jersey: Waldorf School Monographs, 1966.

HANSEN, Hans Helmut: *Die Hiberniaschule und die Durchführung des praktischen Unterrichts - insbesondere der Arbeitslehre - im Zusammenhang ihrer Bildungsarbeit.* Frankfurt/Main: Deutsches Institut für internationale pädagogische Forschung, 1975.

HEYDEBRAND, Caroline: *The Curriculum of the First Waldorf School.* Translated with additional notes on the teaching of English in English schools by E. Hutchines. London: Steiner Schools Fellowship, 1966. rev.

JÜNEMANN, Margrit; WEITMANN, Fritz: *Der künstlerische Unterricht in der Waldorfschule - Malen und Zeichnen.* Stuttgart: Freies Geistesleben; 1976. (Menschenkunde und Erziehung 29).

KETTLE, John: *Waldorf Education for Tomorrow.* Toronto: Waldorf School Association of Ontario, 1968.

KIERSCH, Johannes: *Die Waldorfpädagogik.* Stuttgart: Freies Geistesleben, 1970.

KLOOS, Heinz: *Waldorfpädagogik und Staatsschulwesen.* Stuttgart: Klett, 1955.

KRANICH, Ernst-Michael: *Pädagogische Projekte und ihre Folgen. Zur Problematik von Frühlesenlernen, programmiertem Lernen und neuer Mathematik.* Stuttgart: Freies Geistesleben, 1966.

————: "Die Freien Waldorfschulen". *Freie Schule.* I (1971). (Sonderdruck).

LEBER, Stefan: *Die Sozialgestalt der Waldorfschule. Ein Beitrag zu den sozialwissenschaftlichen Ansichten Rudolf Steiners.* Stuttgart: Freies Geistesleben, 1974. (Menschenkunde und Erziehung 30).

LINDENBERG, Christoph: *Waldorfschulen: angstfrei lernen, selbstbewußt handeln. Praxis eines verkannten Schulmodells.* Reinbek bei Hamburg: Rowohlt Taschenbuch Verlag, 1977. (rororo 6904).

LÜBBERS, Karl-Heinz: *Die Berufsbildung im Rahmen der traditionellen betrieblichen Ausbildung eines Großbetriebes und im System der Hiberniaschule.* Düsseldorf: Deutscher Gewerkschaftsbund, 1972. (Gewerkschaftliche Beiträge zu Fragen der beruflichen Bildung, Broschüre 16).

RAUTHE, Wilhelm: *Die Waldorfschule als Gesamtschule.* Stuttgart: Freies Geistesleben, 1970.

SCHREY, Helmut: *Waldorfpädagogik. Kritische Beschreibung und Versuch eines Gesprächs.* Bonn - Bad Godesberg: Verlag Wissenschaftliches Archiv, 1968.

TAUTZ, Johannes: *Die Freie Waldorfschule. Ursprung und Zielsetzungen.* Stuttgart: Freies Geistesleben, 1972.

*Waldorfpädagogik an öffentlichen Schulen. Versuche und Erfahrungen mit der Pädagogik Rudolf Steiners. Mit vielen Beispielen für eine kindgemäße Unterrichtsgestaltung.* Freiburg: Herder, 1976. (Herderbücherei 9036).

WILKINSON, Roy: *Commonsense Schooling.* East Grinstead, Sussex, England: Henry Goulden, 1975.

3) Periodicals

*Child and Man. A Journal for Contemporary Education.* (Pub. twice yearly). White Heather, Dale Road, Forest Row, Sussex, England.

*Education as an Art.* (Pub. twice yearly by the Waldorf Schools in North America). Anthroposophic Press, Inc., 258 Hungry Hollow Road, Spring Valley, New York 10977, USA.

*Erziehungskunst. Monatsschrift zur Pädagogik Rudolf Steiners.* 41. Jahrgang 1977. Freies Geistesleben, Haussmannstr.76, D 70000 Stuttgart W., Federal Republic of Germany.

*Die Menschenschule. Monatsschrift für Erziehungskunst im Sinne Rudolf Steiners.* 51. Jahrgang 1977. Zbinden Druck und Verlag A.G., Postfach 67, CH 4000s Basel, Switzerland.

*Triades Education.* (Supplement to *Triades Revue de culture humaine*). Centre Triades, 4, rue de la Grande Chaumière, F 75006 Paris, France.

*På Väg mot en ny Pedagogik. Tidskrift för Rudolf Steiner Pedagogik.* Bromma, Sweden.

4) Rudolf Steiner's Writings and Lectures

   a) Original German texts

   - *Rudolf Steiner Gesamtausgabe* (Complete Edition), abbreviated to GA in references. Dornach, Switzerland: Rudolf Steiner Verlag. Begun in 1955 and not yet fully completed.

   - Edition of individual works and pocket books. A complete catalogue of those already available may be obtained from the Rudolf Steiner Verlag. The following is a selection of those directly related to the themes of the present book.

      i) Smaller fundamental texts

      *Die Erziehung des Kindes vom Gesichtspunkte der Geisteswissenschaft* (1907)

      *Das menschliche Leben vom Gesichtspunkte der Geisteswissenschaft (Anthroposophie)* (1916)

      *Reinkarnation und Karma – Wie Karma wirkt* (1903)

*Goethe als Vater einer neuen Aesthetik* (1888)

*Geisteswissenschaft und soziale Frage* (1905/06).

*Die Kardinalfrage des Wirtschaftslebens.* Lecture Oslo 1921.

ii) On education

*Die Erneuerung der pädagogisch-didaktischen Kunst durch Geisteswissenschaft* (1920)

*Die geistig-seelischen Grundkräfte der Erziehungskunst* (1922)

*Gegenwärtiges Geistesleben und Erziehung* (1923)

*Die Kunst des Erziehens aus dem Erfassen der Menschenwesenheit* (1924)

iii) On social themes

*Neuorientierung des Erziehungswesens im Sinne eines freien Geisteslebens. Drei Vorträge über Volkspädagogik* (1919)

*Die Kernpunkte der sozialen Frage in den Lebensnotwendigkeiten der Gegenwart und Zukunft* (1961)

*Aufsätze über die Dreigliederung des sozialen Organismus und zur Zeitlage 1915-1921* (1974)

*Neugestaltung des sozialen Organismus* (1919)

*Gedankenfreiheit und soziale Kräfte. Die sozialen Forderungen der Gegenwart und ihre praktische Verwirklichung* (1919)

*Nationalökonomischer Kurs* (1922)

b) Translations (a selection)

- *Comment acquérir des connaissances sur les mondes supérieurs ou l'initiation.* Paris: Triades, 1976. (Collection de poche "Voie ouverte").
- *Cours sur la culture humaine.* Paris: Triades, 1978.
- *Culture pratique de la pensée, nervosité et le moi, tempéraments.* Genève, Suisse: Editions Anthroposophiques Romandes. (Etudes psychologiques).
- *Discussions with Teachers.* London: Rudolf Steiner Press, 1967.

- *The Education of the Child*. London: Rudolf Steiner Press, 1975.
- *L'éducation de l'enfant à la lumière de la science spirituelle*. Paris: Triades, 1978. (2ième édition).
- *Knowledge of Higher Worlds? How is it Achieved?* London: Rudolf Steiner Press, 1976.
- *The Philosophy of Freedom*. London: Rudolf Steiner Press, 1972.
- *The Philosophy of Spiritual Activity*. West Nyack, New York: Rudolf Steiner Publications, 1963.
- *Practical Advice to Teachers*. London: Rudolf Steiner Press, 1976.
- *Study of Man*. London: Rudolf Steiner Press, 1975.
- *The Supplementary Course*. Forest Row, Sussex, England: Michael Hall School, 1958.
- *Théosophie*. Paris: Triades, 1976. (Collection de poche "Voie ouverte").
- *Theosophie-Theosophy*. Dornach, Switzerland: Rudolf Steiner Verlag, 1975.
- *Theosophy*. London: Rudolf Steiner Press, 1973.